Thank you to all my family whom I work alongside and without whose help having the time to write a book like this would be impossible.

To the invaluable help of Peter Marshall and my editor, designer and all of the publishing team.

A big thank you to Ben and Myburgh for the fabulous photographs.

A huge thank you to Julie Oddie, a most valued member of our team who passes on her chocolate and confectionery skills to all those who attend courses in our school, your input has been invaluable.

Thank you also to Jeanette, Robert and Rob for their chocolate skills. Mark B. for his cake decoration artistry along with Karen and Sarah. Michael for his baking skill and ooh yes, Oliver for his cake pops!

Very big thanks go to all the other members of our team here at Slattery Pâtissier & Chocolatier in Whitefield, who are the best group of people I have ever had the pleasure to work alongside. Their skill as crafts men and women, their patience and customer service are second to none.

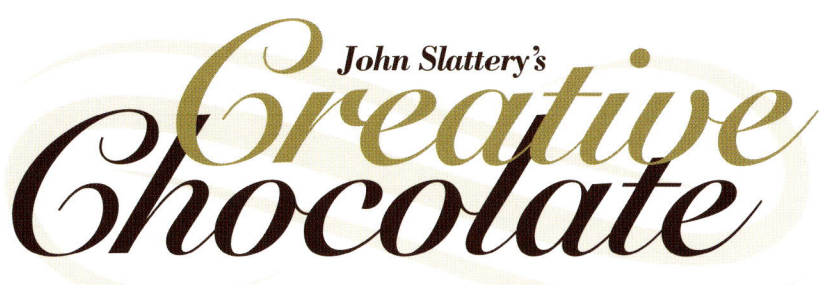

First published in 2011 by Buckingham Book Publishing Ltd
Network House, 28 Ballmoor, Celtic Court,
Buckingham MK18 1RQ, UK
www.chefmagazine.co.uk

© Buckingham Book Publishing Ltd

The rights of the author have been asserted. All rights reserved. No part of this book may be reproduced, stored in a retrieval system or transmitted in any form or by any means, electronic, electrostatic, magnetic tape, mechanical, photocopying, recording or otherwise, without the prior permission in writing of the publisher.

ISBN No: 978-1-908202-07-9

Publisher: Peter Marshall
Managing Editor: Shirley Marshall
Editor: Katy Morris
Recipe Editor: Sue Christelow
Editorial Assistant: Danielle May
Design Director: Philip Donnelly
Graphic Designer: Duncan Boddy
Photographers: Myburgh du Plessis, Ben Pollard

Introduction

John Slattery has always been a little in love with chocolate – eating it, cooking with it, creating with it – for John, chocolate can be used to create a million possibilities.

Having worked in baking and confectionery all his life and being part of the family business for over 40 years, spending every day with his favourite ingredient was a natural move. Having trained at college John has also attended courses in the chocolate capitals of the world; Switzerland, Belgium and Austria among others, gaining both skills and experience. His passion for chocolate is clear as John is a member of the British Confectioners Association, The National Association of Master Bakers and the International Richemont Club – a centre for master bakers and confectioners.

Now John shares his love of chocolate with others, in the form of Slattery Pâtissier & Chocolatier Ltd, a chocolate shop based on Bury New Road in Whitefield, Manchester. Affectionately known as 'that wicked shop', this unique store specialises in celebration cakes, chocolate treats and prides itself on being able to create anything in chocolate! Of course, hand-made chocolates and chocolate gifts are also available with a dining room above offering breakfast, lunch and afternoon tea.

John also offers a variety of courses in chocolate, cake decorating and other confectionery on the third floor of the shop, otherwise known as The School of Excellence. It is here that he and his staff meet many chocolate lovers that wish to advance their skills but have always found the practice of making chocolate creations overwhelming.

John Slattery's *Creative Chocolate* will help beginners release their chocolate-making potential so that they can really make the most of this luxurious ingredient. The clear step-by-step instructions and helpful tips make even the most show-stopping of desserts an ease to create. With John's expert knowledge of pâtisserie, bakery and confectionery, all basic aspects of chocolate work are covered, including tempering and using moulds. Plus his techniques are revealed as he explains how to create basic cakes, ganaches and other toppings as well as how to layer and decorate so that readers can be confident that their creation will be the talk of the table.

And for those that just fancy something little to satisfy their chocolate craving, the sweet treats and tart recipes are sure to keep everyone occupied. If you are looking for something a little more advanced the chocolate desserts and tarts are great for dinner parties (if you can bear to share them). Together with a comprehensive glossary and equipment index you really can release your inner chocolatier.

After all, the art of chocolate doesn't need to be just for experts – unwrap your chocolate potential with John's inspirational and delicious recipes and give in to your love of chocolate with *Creative Chocolate!*

Please note the oven temperatures in this book are in Celsius and measured in metric with cake sizes in cm – although there is an inches reference in the quantity matrix at the back of the book. Cocoa percentage is referenced where necessary and chocolate used is always broken into small pieces or in button/drop form for ease of melting.

Contents

Introduction – 02

A History of Chocolate – 06

Types of Chocolate – 08

SWEETS AND TREATS – 10

Cake Pops – 12

Manchester Tart Chocolates – 16

Chocolate Baubles – 20

PCP (Pine Nut, Cranberry and Praline) – 24

White Chocolate Fudge – 26

Fruit and Nut Tiffin – 28

TARTS AND PASTRIES – 30

Chocolate Pecan Pie – 32

Manchester Tart with a Chocolate Twist – 34

Chocolate Tarts – 36

Strawberry Shortbread Hearts – 40

Chocolate and Raspberry Cardinal – 44

DESSERTS – 48

Chocolate and Pear, Bread and Butter Pudding – 50

Chocolate and Toffee Soufflé – 52

Chocolate Nemesis – 54

Double Chocolate Baked Cheesecake – 58

Spiced Chocolate Pudding – 60

Chocolate and Kumquat Semi-Freddo – 64

CAKES – 68

Drunken Chocolate Cake – 70

Chocolate Torte – 72

Chocolate and Coffee Cake – 76

Chocolate Cupcakes – 80

Chocolate Pecan Brownies – 84

CENTREPIECE CAKES – 86

Agni – 88

Andora – 92

Bubble – 96

Fiona – 101

Georgia – 104

Julie – 108

Lola – 112

Olivia – 116

Suzie – 120

Tiffany – 126

Zandra – 130

Darcy – 134

Shardé – 141

A GUIDE TO… – 144

Equipment – 146

Melting and Tempering – 150

Using Moulds – 154

Base Cakes – 156

Filling – 158

Layering – 160

Covering with Marzipan – 162

Levelling – 163

Dowelling – 164

Textures and Curls – 165

Glossary – 166

Quantities Matrix – 167

Templates – 168

Suppliers – 173

Index – 174

The History of Chocolate

The chocolate story can be traced as far back as 1502 – when Christopher Columbus landed on the isle of Guanaja off the coast of Honduras, he was given a gift of cocoa beans.

But it was not until 17 years later that Hernán Cortés landed on the present day Mexico where he embarked on his conquest of the Aztec empire. He met the famous emperor Montezuma, whose love of cocoa is legendary – almost as well known as his harem of 365 brides. Believing in the aphrodisiac quality of cocoa, the emperor reputedly drank up to 50 cups a day of Xocoatl (a drink based on cocoa, water, maize meal, vanilla and chilli) – a far cry from the chocolate we know and love.

It was with Cortés that the development of chocolate began. On discovering that they were equivalent to currency he shipped the cacao beans – 'the gold of the New World' – back to Spain to be planted. The drink – still too bitter for European taste – was adapted with sugar and made more palatable although this was an exclusive luxury for the super-rich and royalty. However, times changed and a century later chocolate was first unveiled to the masses with chocolate houses becoming the ultimate trend for the upper classes.

By the 17th century milk had been added and the mix acknowledged as 'drinking chocolate' – this recipe was adapted and thus non-liquid chocolate was created – therefore creating the very first bar. Now using a conching to bind cocoa butter, cocoa solids and sugar together the Victorian era became a time of change for chocolate as plantations grew and industry was revolutionised. Today the production is very similar with methods in place to control the quality, flavour and type of chocolate produced – quite a voyage for a little bean from Central America!

Types of Chocolate

Chocolate is made by roasting cocoa beans and grinding and heating the kernels to produce cocoa mass and cocoa butter.

For dark chocolate, cocoa mass, cocoa butter and sometimes a little sugar are mixed together to form a dough. After intensive mixing, this dough is refined by rollers. The dough is then rolled and refined to produce a very fine chocolate powder. It is at this point that, by varying the balance of ingredients, different chocolate types and flavours are created, before being turned into liquid ready to form into blocks or callets (drops). For milk chocolate, milk solids are added and for white chocolate, extra cocoa butter, extra sugar and milk solids replace the cocoa solids.

Making and decorating cakes using chocolate is a real craft and you need to make sure that you are working with the best type of chocolate, known as couverture. Belgian chocolate is well known for its consistent quality and is ideal for the cakes in this book. Its high cocoa butter content and absence of added fat make it a beautifully rich but easily workable medium. Use the chocolate in block or drop form. Cooking chocolate is easy to use for pouring over cakes and it does not require tempering, but there is no comparison when it comes to taste. Although any good quality chocolate can be used this book uses chocolate callets from Barry Callebaut. For further information please visit www.barry-callebaut.com or call Slattery's for more information.

SWEETS & TREATS

Cake Pops

MAKES 50

The idea of presenting a small cake on a stick is one of those ideas that you wish you had thought up, but sadly I cannot claim this one. To take a concept and add your own inspiration and flair is to help with its progression. So here's my take on the 'cake pop'. Using good quality chocolate both inside and for the decoration makes this item more appreciated by a 'grown-up' audience also.

Roll the cake pop mix into 40g balls

With tempered chocolate secure the stick into the position in the ball

Dip the chilled ball in tempered chocolate

INGREDIENTS

1kg Off-cuts of cake

400g Jam

400g Buttercream

200g Desired chocolate, tempered

METHOD

1. Reduce the cake to crumbs using a mixer with a hook attachment on first speed.
2. Add the jam and buttercream, mixing to a smooth paste. Scrape down the bowl. Depending on the moistness of the cake used you may need to adjust the consistency here by adding a little more crumb.
3. Mix in the chocolate. A quick burst on second speed aids this process.
4. Place the mix into a plastic bag and refrigerate.
5. When firm roll out lengths 'sausage' style. Divide into small equal pieces of approximately 40g each. Roll into balls and place onto a plastic covered tray. Refrigerate again for a few minutes.
6. Take a small bowl of tempered chocolate. Dip the stick in the chocolate to just over 1cm deep. Push the dipped end into the 'pop' about two-thirds of the way. Place on a tray and keep refrigerated until you are ready for dipping.
7. Prepare tempered chocolate, dark, milk or white or add colour or flavour to the chocolate to create the desired effect on the finished product. Dip and enjoy!

CAKE POPS

For round 'pops', the additions of sparkles, sprinkles and textures complete the finished product. When dipping the 'pop' in the chocolate, remove the excess by touching the surface of the chocolate in the bowl several times to avoid drips etc.

The recipe when chilled allows for the creation of shaped 'pops', either forming by hand, or using cutters or moulds to press the mix into.

With this in mind the possibilities are limited only by your imagination to create 'pops' for different occasions and the seasons of the year.

The other option of course is flavour. By using different types of cake, the colour, taste and texture can be altered. By replacing the jam and buttercream with alternatives eg. lemon curd, marmalade or fudges, additional flavour combinations can also be achieved.

Ginger, strawberry, lemon, peanut butter, orange, chocolate, perhaps 'grown-up' flavours with the addition of alcohol, gin and tonic, rum and blackcurrant or cocktails eg. Strawberry Daiquiri or Peach Bellini. The list can go on and on thus giving a whole new meaning to the word ' alcopop'.

Orange cake, orange curd, buttercream, white chocolate, sugar sprinkles.

Chocolate cake, chocolate ganache, milk chocolate, with chocolate coated crunchy biscuit.

A 'grown up' pop; vanilla sponge, lime marmalade, buttercream, white rum, a little strawberry liquor dipped in a strawberry flavour chocolate.

Another 'alcopop' using chocolate cake, dark rum, blackcurrant jam, buttercream coated with smooth white chocolate.

Lemon cake, tangy lemon curd, buttercream, white chocolate, and lemon sugar crystals.

Vanilla sponge, cherry jam, buttercream, white chocolate and decorated mini marshmallows.

An extra 'pop' can be achieved by incorporating the cake pops with 'popping candy' or with stylish silver balls.

Fruit cocktail; into a basic mix of sponge, jam and cream incorporate some diced crystallised fruit pieces or jelly beans, this is reflected in the decoration on the outside.

Ginger cake softened with ginger wine bound together with apricot jam and a little buttercream, or try your prefered chocolate dipped with 'hundreds and thousands'.

Strawberry jelly pieces mixed into a vanilla cake, strawberry jam and buttercream coated in milk chocolate and decorated with strawberry chocolate drops.

Manchester Tart Chocolates

MAKES 36 CHOCOLATES

Manchester Tart Chocolates

The 'Manchester Tart' is a revival of a traditional pudding, mentioned by Mrs Beeton in her famous cookery books, but more fondly remembered from the school dinners of the 50s and 60s. This is a modern twist recreating the flavours in a small chocolate, perfect for after dinner.

INGREDIENTS

250g Milk chocolate required (up to 1kg to work with)

75g Raspberry jam (of good quality)

75g Desiccated coconut

'Custard' Filling – White Chocolate Ganache:

135g Whipping cream

35g Liquid glucose

3 drops Vanilla compound*

10g Custard powder

270g White chocolate

* Vanilla compound – use a good quality concentrated vanilla.

METHOD

1. Mould a chocolate case in milk chocolate (I have used 'chocolate world' mould number 1241) see using moulds page 154. Allow to set.
2. Although each empty chocolate case weighs only 7g remember you will need to temper additional chocolate to allow for filling the moulds, emptying and working with the chocolate – the excess can be used again.
3. Pipe a generous bulb (2g) of raspberry jam into the base of each set chocolate case.

'Custard' Filling – White Chocolate Ganache

1. Bring to the boil the cream and the glucose with the vanilla, then whisk in the custard powder.
2. Pour onto the chocolate, leave for 1 minute and then stir to combine the ingredients.
3. Stir occasionally until all the chocolate is melted
4. Leave to cool completely (better to cover with plastic to prevent skinning). I find it better to make this the day before and allow to stand overnight at room temperature.
5. Put the ganache into the machine bowl of an electric mixer fitted with a beater, then aerate on medium speed for approximately 4 minutes.
6. Put the ganache in a Savoy piping bag fitted with a 7/8cm plain tube (nozzle).
7. Pipe the ganache to seal over the jam in the base and fill just over the brim of the chocolate case.
8. Sprinkle with desiccated coconut.
9. Allow to set.

These chocolates are best enjoyed eaten fresh, because the ganache filling is exposed (not sealed in with chocolate to protect it) and the air will dry it out. Store in a dark airtight container and eat within 3 weeks.

Chocolate Baubles

MAKES 12

Chocolate Baubles

Piled on a stand as a wedding cake to create a stunning centrepiece for any celebration these chocolate baubles look fab. Individually boxed they make a super Christmas table gift to delight your guests.

INGREDIENTS

20cm Sponge cake (see recipe matrix page 167)

480g Desired chocolate required (rounded up to 600g to work with)

Milk Chocolate Ganache:

400g Whipping cream

100g Liquid glucose

800g Milk chocolate

If you wish to embellish further, once set the chocolate piping can be brushed with edible gold or silver lustre.

Cut chocolate cake rounds, slice into thin discs

Pipe and layer ganache into a half sphere

Layer with a round of cake

'Glue' the two halves together

METHOD

Using a 7cm half sphere mould create some half ball shapes in chocolate, milk, white or dark. Ensure the chocolate is not too thick so they eat well, but avoid being too thin so you can handle them. (See use of moulds page 154).

Out of a sheet of chocolate sponge cake, cut some circles using 6cm and 4cm metal cutters. Slice each of these into approximately 7mm thin discs. You will need one disc of each size to layer each half sphere. Chocolate cake recipe (see page 156).

Milk Chocolate Ganache:

1. Bring to the boil the cream and the glucose.
2. Pour onto the chocolate, leave for 1 minute and then stir to combine the ingredients.
3. Stir occasionally until all the chocolate is melted.
4. Leave to cool completely (better to cover with plastic to prevent skinning). I find it better to make this the day before and allow to stand overnight at room temperature.
5. Put the ganache into the machine bowl of an electric mixer fitted with a beater, then aerate on medium speed for approximately 5 minutes
6. Put some of the ganache in a piping bag fitted with a 1cm plain tube (nozzle).

Assembly:

1. Pipe a small bulb of ganache into each half sphere, top this with the smaller disc of sponge, pipe a thin layer of ganache and top with the second larger disc of sponge; a thin scraping of ganache on top of this seals the cake but also acts as the glue to help join the two halves of the sphere together. Pipe a thin line of tempered chocolate on the edge of one half sphere and join firmly together to create a whole ball. Wipe away any excess chocolate from the join. A little practice can ensure this can be reduced to a minimum. When handling chocolate this way you are best wearing fine cotton or latex gloves so as not to mark with fingerprints etc.
2. To create a base for the baubles to sit on, pipe a bulb of tempered chocolate onto a piece of plastic, allow it to start to set and put the chocolate bauble on.
3. The baubles can then be decorated by piping chocolate in lines, loops, dots or filigree to create a pleasing effect (a paper piping bag with a number 1 or 1.5 plain tube [nozzle] is used for this).
4. If you wish to embellish further, once set the chocolate piping can be brushed with edible gold or silver lustre.

P.C.P. – Pine Nut, Cranberry and Praline

MAKES 20 SLICES

Such a simple way to create a delicious sweet treat. Perfect as an after dinner chocolate.

INGREDIENTS

400g Praline paste
200g Milk chocolate, tempered
100g Feuilletine
35g Toasted pine nuts
25g Dried cranberries
100g Milk chocolate, tempered, for decoration

This recipe can also be formed into a sheet. Cut into small squares and then fully enrobe in chocolate.

METHOD

1. Combine all the ingredients except the chocolate together.
2. Leave to firm slightly.
3. Deposit onto two 38cm squares of cling film.
4. Roll up to form 'sausages' 20-23cm in length.
5. Refrigerate for at least 2 hours to allow to firm up.
6. Unroll, remove and discard the cling film.
7. Coat with milk chocolate using a knife or brush to form a 'tree bark' effect.
8. Present in cut slices – delicious!

To create a contrast use dark chocolate to coat the roll with, white chocolate can look particularly festive. And of course the inclusions can be swapped about to form different initials …

W.P.C. Walnut, Praline Cashew
R.B.P. Raisin, Brazil, Praline
G.P.H. Ginger, Praline, Hazel

The possibilities are limited only by your imagination and good taste.

White Chocolate Fudge

MAKES 100 SQUARES

Ooh so simple... but ooh so good!
Everybody's favourite... as long as it has chocolate on!

INGREDIENTS

600g Caster sugar
225g Liquid glucose
225g Unsalted butter, diced
550g Whipping cream
50g Vanilla paste
500g White chocolate

Decoration:

150g White chocolate, tempered
15g Milk chocolate, tempered and in a piping bag

METHOD

1. Bring slowly up to the boil all the ingredients except the chocolate – boil to 120°C (hard ball stage).
2. Lift off the heat and mix in the chocolate.
3. Pour onto a cling film lined tray 12 x 38cm.
4. Allow to set.
5. When completely cold and firm coat the top with a thin layer of white chocolate.
6. Remove from the tray and discard the cling film.
7. Coat the other side with a thin layer of white chocolate and decorate with a swirl of milk chocolate to form the top of the product.
8. Cut into small squares.

This fudge will keep for a month if you keep it airtight or if you can keep your hands off it that long!

The basic recipe may be used, substituting milk or dark chocolate to create contrasting varieties.

MAKES 64

Fruit and Nut Tiffin

A variation of the good old fashioned 'refrigerator cake', tiffin has become a firm family favourite of ours over the years, simple to make and always a 'crowd pleaser'.

INGREDIENTS

500g Golden syrup

500g Caramel

1kg Unsalted butter

3kg Digestive biscuit crumbs

400g Sultanas

400g Raisins

400g Glacé cherries

200g Walnut halves

200g Pecan halves

200g Roasted hazelnuts

200g Brazil nuts chopped

2kg Dark chocolate (70%), melted

METHOD

1. Warm together the syrup, caramel and butter.
2. Add to the digestive crumbs and part mix.
3. Add all the fruit and nuts and part mix again.
4. Add the melted chocolate and mix completely together.
5. Pour onto a greaseproof paper lined tray, 76 x 46cm.
6. Allow to set in the fridge until firm.
7. Cut into fingers or squares.
8. Squares can be coated on the base with chocolate, fully enrobed or just spun with chocolate to decorate as desired.

This recipe keeps well and is versatile as it can be presented as a cake slice finger. Cut small it makes a good 'mini bite' or cut even smaller it can make a great addition to your petit four range.

Remember all the fruit and nut content in this recipe can be substituted (like-for-like) with your favourite inclusions, for example mini marshmallow, glacé cherries or orange peel, diced preserved ginger or M&M's® – the list is endless.

TARTS & PASTRIES

MAKES 20 TARTS

Chocolate Pecan Pie

It's true that 'most things taste better with chocolate, in the case of this pecan pie 'doubly good' as we have incorporated chocolate in both the pastry and the delicious filling.

INGREDIENTS

Chocolate pastry:
175g Plain flour
25g Cocoa powder
125g Margarine or butter
50g Caster sugar
2 Egg yolks
30g Water

Chocolate pecan filling:
350g Caster sugar
300g Maple or golden syrup
100g Butter
85g Cocoa powder
6 Eggs
8g Vanilla
400g Pecan nuts, chopped
Pecan halves for decoration (3 halves for each)
Apricot glaze, to finish

METHOD

Chocolate pastry:
1. Sieve the flour and cocoa powder together.
2. Rub in the fat.
3. Dissolve the sugar in the egg yolks and water, add to the mix and make up into a paste.
4. Refrigerate for at least 10 minutes to rest.
5. Block into foil cases or hand-lined tins (we use a 10cm tin foil case with a fluted crimp).

Chocolate pecan filling:
1. Warm and dissolve together the sugar, syrup and butter.
2. Add the cocoa powder, eggs and vanilla.
3. Stir in the chopped pecans.
4. Deposit the filling (70g) into the prepared pastry cases (10cm).
5. Decorate the top with three nuts halves.
6. Bake at 190°C for 20 minutes.
7. Glaze when cool with an apricot glaze to seal the tart.

The filling can be made in a larger quantity and stored in a sealed container in the refrigerator for up to 2 weeks. Fresh tarts can be baked each day from this recipe (stir well each day before use as the mix tends to separate with standing).

Manchester Tart with a Chocolate Twist

MAKES 10 TARTS

This is a twist on the traditional Manchester tart, much beloved in its 'heyday' in the 1970s and 80s when it featured on the school dinner menu.

INGREDIENTS

Pastry:

500g Butter or margarine

200g Caster sugar

4 Whole eggs (medium)

700g Plain flour

Filling:

3 Whole eggs (medium)

120g Caster sugar

10g Vanilla paste

40g Cornflour

640g Full-fat milk

100g Dark chocolate (70%)

Fruit jam or Nutella, to finish

Chocolate flakes or other chocolate decoration

METHOD

Pastry:

1. Cream together the butter and sugar.
2. Add the eggs one at a time.
3. Add the sieved flour and bring to a paste without working it too much.
4. Wrap in plastic and chill/rest in the refrigerator for at least 30 minutes.
5. Using a rolling pin on a lightly floured surface roll out the pastry and line small tart cases, allowing them to rest back in the refrigerator to avoid shrinkage.
6. Bake blind at 180°C for approximately 10 minutes.

Filling:

1. Make a custard by whisking the eggs, sugar, vanilla and cornflour together.
2. Bring the milk to the boil.
3. Add to the combined ingredients.
4. Return all to the pan and cook for a few minutes, whisking all the time.
5. Remove from the heat.
6. Add the chocolate, stirring well until dissolved.
7. Deposit a little fruit jam or Nutella onto the baked pastry.
8. Pour the chocolate custard over this, allowing it to cool completely.
9. Add some chocolate flakes or other desired chocolate decoration to finish.

For an imaginative twist, try adding fresh fruit, several work well but fresh strawberries are particularly delicious. Over a thin layer of strawberry jam in the base place a few strawberry halves, then cover with the custard. Finish this with a strawberry half dipped in chocolate.

Chocolate Tarts

MAKES 15

Chocolate Tart

A rich decadent confection, perfect for dinner parties and after dinner occasions. Decorate to your own taste with fruit, chocolate curls or biscuits – or enjoy on its own for a luxurious chocolate treat.

INGREDIENTS

Pastry:

A good 'short eating' sweet pastry to line or block into foil cases (see recipe for the Chocolate and Raspberry Cardinal on page 44)

Filling:

450ml Whipping cream

400ml Full-fat milk

250g Dark chocolate (70% or above)

10 Egg yolks

135g Caster sugar

METHOD

Filling:

1. Bring the cream and milk to the boil.
2. Melt the chocolate.
3. Whisk the chocolate into the milk and cream mixture.
4. Mix together the egg yolks and sugar.
5. Pour the hot chocolate cream mixture over the eggs and sugar mix.
6. Return to the pan and bring back to the boil, whisking all the time.
7. This mix can be used straight away or may be cooled and refrigerated in a sealed container until required.
8. Lightly part bake the pastry cases.
9. Pipe the filling into the pastry cases (with a slight dome) – the yield is 30 x 10cm rounds or 4 x 25cm rounds.
10. Bake at 170°C for 25 minutes until set.
11. Allow to cool completely before adding chocolate decorations as desired.

Release your creative side by replacing the dark chocolate with white or caramel. Or we do a delicious 'chocolate orange tart' with the addition of a tangy orange curd in the base before the chocolate filling is piped in.

MAKES 45

Strawberry Shortbread Hearts

A delicious combination of chocolate and fresh fruit that is equally at home as the finale for an alfresco BBQ or as the centrepiece for a summer wedding.

INGREDIENTS

Shortbread:

950g Butter
390g Caster sugar
1345g Soft flour
50g Rice flour

White chocolate ganache:

400g Whipping cream
100g Liquid glucose
800g White chocolate

Decoration:

45 Strawberries
White chocolate, tempered
Milk chocolate, tempered

METHOD

Shortbread:

1. All ingredients should be at room temperature.
2. Cream the butter and sugar together until light and fluffy.
3. Sieve the flour and rice flour together.
4. Fold into the creamed butter and sugar and mix until a smooth 'dough' is formed, wrap in a plastic bag and refrigerate for at least 1 hour. The dough can be stored for up to 1 week in the fridge.
5. On a lightly floured surface (or you can use rice cones) roll out the shortbread with a rolling pin; spacer bars can be used to ensure an even thickness of 1cm is achieved.
6. Cut out heart shapes to the desired size (shown here approximately 5cm across).
7. Bake at 190°C for approximately 12 minutes, then allow to cool completely.
8. Dip half of the biscuits halfway in dark chocolate and then the remaining opposite half in milk chocolate.

White chocolate ganache:

1. Bring to the boil the cream and the glucose.
2. Pour onto the chocolate, leave for 1 minute and then stir to combine the ingredients.
3. Stir occasionally until all the chocolate has melted.
4. Leave to cool completely (it is best to cover with plastic to prevent skinning). I find it better to make this the day before and allow it to stand overnight at room temperature.
5. Put the ganache into the machine bowl of an electric mixer fitted with a beater and aerate on medium speed for approximately 5 minutes.
6. Put some of the ganache in a piping bag fitted with a 1cm plain tube nozzle.
7. Lay out 45 of the half-dipped biscuits and pipe three bulbs of ganache on to each (approximately 30g total).
8. Top each with a second dipped biscuit, pushing down gently to ensure the top biscuit holds in place; with this action you can also press out the ganache a little to ensure they all look even.

Decoration:

1. The strawberry placed on top can either be dipped in tempered white chocolate and decorated by 'spinning' piping some fine lines of milk chocolate across each – place in position so the chocolate sets to hold the fruit in place.
2. An alternative decoration can be achieved by piping the fine lines of milk chocolate on to the surface of a bowl of white chocolate and then dipping the strawberry into this, thus creating lines or a marble decoration on each fruit. Two or three fruits can be dipped and then repipe the fine milk chocolate lines.

Chocolate and Raspberry Cardinal

SERVES 10

Chocolate and Raspberry Cardinal

Certainly gets a big oooh! At a dinner party this easily created dessert has a taste to match it's good looks.

INGREDIENTS

Sweet pastry:
100g Caster sugar
250g Unsalted butter
2 Whole eggs
350g Plain flour
Melted chocolate or cocoa butter, for brushing
Fresh raspberries

Ganache:
250g Whipping cream
25g Liquid glucose
200g Dark chocolate (70%), chopped
80g Unsalted butter

Decoration:
Fresh raspberries
Chocolate ruffles

METHOD

Sweet pastry:
1. Mix the sugar and butter (at room temperature) together.
2. Add the eggs.
3. Add the sieved flour and bring to a paste without overworking.
4. Place into a plastic bag or wrap in cling film.
5. Refrigerate for at least 30 minutes.
6. Roll out the pastry using a minimum of flour.
7. Line a flan tin or dish with the pastry 23cm.
8. Place into the refrigerator to rest before baking to prevent shrinkage.
9. Bake blind using baking beans at 180°C for 10 to 15 minutes.
10. Once the pastry base is cool, brush the inside with melted chocolate or cocoa butter to prevent it becoming soggy.
11. Cover the base with the raspberries.

Ganache:
1. Bring the cream and glucose to the boil.
2. Pour onto the chopped chocolate.
3. Mix until smooth.
4. Allow to cool then mix in the butter.
5. Pour over the raspberries and allow to set.
6. Decorate with fresh raspberries and chocolate ruffles.

The chocolate ruffles are created by spreading melted chocolate onto a frozen marble slab using a 'wall paper' style scraper with a handle. The chocolate sets straight away, cut into strips with the corner of the scraper, slide the scraper to release from the slab and manipulate and fold into a ruffle. Speed is important here and I would suggest a little practice wouldn't go amiss.

DESSERTS

Chocolate and Pear Bread and Butter Pudding

SERVES 12

Chocolate and pear have often been 'dessert partners'. This recipe creates a hot eating pudding where the intense chocolate notes are balanced by soft, smooth fruit.

INGREDIENTS

400g Dark chocolate (70%)

150g Butter

220g Caster sugar

850g Whipping cream

6 Whole eggs

2 pinches Cinnamon

400g 3-day-old bread, sliced and crusts removed (500g loaf with the crusts removed)

4 Pears, peeled, poached and sliced into wedges (tinned pears can be used)

METHOD

1. Melt together the chocolate, butter, sugar and cream in a plastic bowl in the microwave.
2. Whisk the eggs together with the cinnamon and add to the above mix.
3. Cut the bread into small squares or triangles and dip each piece into the mix, allowing a few seconds to absorb the custard.
4. Arrange into oven-proof containers interspersing with the drained sliced pears (either individual ramekins or larger dishes for multiple portions).
5. Pour over any remaining custard.
6. Bake at 180°C for 30 to 40 minutes (it is ready when it springs back when you press the middle, like a sponge cake).
7. Serve hot or cold.

While I prefer to use plain white bread in this recipe because it is less sweet you can use brioche or panettone to create a softer, sweeter eat. I prefer this pudding served hot accompanied with a poached pear and a pool of fresh cream (as illustrated). However, if you assemble and bake it in a shallow dish and allow it to cool completely the pudding can be cut into small cubes or triangles and served as a canapé dessert or as part of a trio of mini chocolate desserts served together.

Chocolate and Toffoc Soufflé

MAKES 10

What better combination than chocolate with a smooth caramel toffee, Toffoc is a toffee vodka from Wales which manages to release a smooth flavour with a kick!

INGREDIENTS

Pastry cream:

4 Egg yolks
50g Caster sugar
30g Plain flour
250g Full-fat milk
1 Vanilla pod
40g Toffoc Vodka
(delicious toffee vodka)

Meringue:

8 Egg whites
150g Caster sugar
80g Dark chocolate
(70% or above), chopped

METHOD

Pastry cream:

1. Mix the egg yolks, sugar and flour together.
2. Boil the milk and vanilla.
3. Pour onto the yolk mixture and whisk well together.
4. Return to the pan until the sauce thickens, whisking all the time.
5. Pour into a clean bowl and place cling film over the surface to prevent a skin forming.
6. Allow the pastry cream to cool a little then mix in the liqueur.

Meringue:

1. Whisk the egg whites until fluffy.
2. Add the sugar to produce a firm meringue.
3. Add a little of the meringue into the pastry cream and mix until smooth.
4. Fold in the remaining meringue and chocolate.
5. Place into buttered and floured ramekins, fill to the top and place on a baking tray.
6. Bake in a hot oven at 210°C for 7 to 10 minutes.
7. On removal from the oven dust with icing sugar and serve immediately.

Whilst I think the Toffoc is ideal in this recipe the alcohol can be changed to suite your palate, Grand Marnier or Cointreau being more traditional.

Chocolate Nemesis

Chocolate Nemesis

SERVES 10

Our take on what has become a classic. A chocolate dessert served hot with smooth ice cream is a delicious pudding. But this 'nemesis' has a taste and texture that you will be in danger of being 'beaten by'.

INGREDIENTS

5 Whole eggs
100g Caster sugar
180g Caster sugar
125g Water
335g Dark chocolate (70% or above), melted
225g Unsalted butter

To serve:
Vanilla ice cream

METHOD

1. Whisk the eggs and 100g sugar together for 10 minutes.
2. Boil the 180g sugar and water together to 118°C.
3. Pour the boiled sugar into the egg mix.
4. Whisk until smooth.
5. Fold in the chocolate and butter.
6. Mix until smooth.
7. Pour the mix into ramekins.
8. Bake at 150°C for 45 to 50 minutes.
9. Serve with vanilla ice cream.

In the famous recipe from the 'River Café' this dessert is baked in a water bath, following the above recipe gives a more open texture to the cake which I think is preferable when served warm. Serve with a shot of chocolate sauce for added luxury.

Double Chocolate Baked Cheesecake

MAKES 30

This recipe the basis of which I collected on a visit to New York, gives you a fail safe delicious to eat confection, that never fails to please.

INGREDIENTS

Filling:

1kg Full-fat cream cheese
250g Caster sugar
55g Cornflour
150g Fresh whole eggs
530g Whipping cream
400g White chocolate
200g Dark chocolate (70%)

Base:

70g Golden syrup
70g Unsalted butter
390g Digestive biscuit crumbs

METHOD

Filling:

1. Using a beater on slow speed, mix together the cream cheese, sugar and cornflour.
2. Add the eggs over 1 minute.
3. Now exchange the beater for the whisk and on second speed whisk until smooth.
4. Slowly add the cream while scraping down the bowl twice.
5. Put half the mix into another bowl.
6. Add the white chocolate to one half and the dark chocolate to the other.
7. Mix until clear.

Base:

1. Melt together the golden syrup and butter and mix into the digestive crumb.
2. Place 26g of mix into a 7½cm diameter hoop placed on a silicone sheet on a baking tray. Press the crumb mix down firmly.
3. Place the cheesecake into two piping bags and deposit equal amounts of each flavour side by side into the hoops.
4. With a circular motion using a skewer, create a marble effect on the top.
5. Bake at 160°C for 35 to 40 minutes.
6. Probe the centre of the cheesecakes – they should reach 72°C.
7. Once baked this cheesecake can be frozen if required.

Spiced Chocolate Pudding

Spiced Chocolate Pudding

SERVES 10

This pudding with its molten centre, is a truly irresistible infusion of spices and chocolate.

INGREDIENTS

300g Dark chocolate (70% or above)
250g Unsalted butter
4 Egg yolks
8 Whole eggs
260g Caster sugar
120g Plain flour
20g Cocoa powder
20g Mixed spice

METHOD

1. Melt the chocolate and butter.
2. Whisk the yolks, whole eggs and sugar to the thick ribbon stage to make a sabayon.
3. Mix the sabayon with the melted chocolate and butter.
4. Sieve the flour, cocoa powder and mixed spice into the above and fold in.
5. Pour into greased dariole moulds, three-quarters full.
6. Bake at 350°C for 15 to 20 minutes.
7. This mix can be frozen in the moulds and baked from frozen. Allow a little extra time in the oven, 25 to 30 minutes.

Serve with a swirl of mango coulis and a scoop of vanilla ice cream to complement this delicious warm pud.

Chocolate and Kumquat Semi-Freddo

Chocolate and Kumquat Semi-Freddo

SERVES 10

A sophisticated dessert requiring advance preparation, but the result justifies the effort. Rich and decadent.

INGREDIENTS

Honey Anglaise:
800g Double cream
24 Egg yolks
200g Caster sugar
400g Honey

Ganache:
400g Double cream
600g Dark chocolate (70%)

Compote:
250g Kumquats
250g Caster sugar
250g Water
1 Cinnamon stick

To serve:
Toblerone, chopped
Pistachio nuts, chopped

METHOD

Honey Anglaise:
1. Boil the cream.
2. Mix together the egg yolks, sugar and honey.
3. Pour the cream onto the yolks and sugar, return to a clean pan and cook slowly, over a low heat, stirring all the time. The crème Anglaise will thicken but must not boil.

Ganache:
1. Boil the cream and pour over the broken chocolate.
2. Mix to a smooth ganache.
3. Mix the ganache into the honey Anglaise.
4. Cover with cling film to avoid skinning.
5. Chill overnight.

Compote:
1. Trim the ends off the kumquats and leave whole.
2. Place in a pan with the sugar and water.
3. Simmer until the liquid reduces down.
4. Allow to cool.

Assembly:
1. Layer a terrine with the chocolate Anglaise mix and alternate layers of chopped Toblerone and pistachio nuts.
2. Freeze until set.
3. Turn out and slice. Serve with the compote of kumquats.

In the photo opposite, the top decoration is created by piping chocolate in a circular motion onto coloured sugar, when it's set shake off the excess and place in position.

CAKES

Drunken Chocolate Cake

SERVES 12

This is one of those recipes that tastes far better than it reads. It creates a rich, moist dessert that if served with a dollop of fresh whipped cream is a simple but elegant finale to any meal.

INGREDIENTS

500g Chocolate cake, broken into small pieces

300g Brandy

500g Digestive biscuits, broken

400g Fresh whipping cream

1.2kg Dark Chocolate

Decoration:

200g Digestive biscuit crumbs, sieved to remove fine particles

METHOD

1. Prepare a 25cm cake hoop by sitting it on to a plastic sheet on a metal tray. Line around the inside of the hoop with a strip of acetate.
2. Place the chocolate cake pieces into a bowl, add the brandy and allow to absorb. Stir occasionally to ensure all the cake is moist.
3. Add the broken digestive biscuits and mix in.
4. Bring the cream to the boil and pour onto the chocolate. Stir to allow the heat from the cream to melt the chocolate.
5. When a smooth ganache is achieved, add this to the other ingredients and mix thoroughly.
6. Pour the mix into the prepared cake hoop.
7. Place into the refrigerator overnight.
8. Remove from the refrigerator, remove the metal hoop and peel away the acetate strip.

Decoration:

1. Using a heat gun (or a hair dryer) warm the surface of the cake.
2. Press the biscuit crumbs around the sides and over the top.
3. Mark with the back of a knife blade into portions.

The brandy can be substituted for most other spirits or liquors; Amaretto, Grand Marnier, Baileys Irish Cream or a mellow whisky all work well.

The flavour of this cake improves with allowing to mature for a day or two in an airtight container in a cool place, before final decoration and serving.

SERVES 10

Chocolate Torte

A traditional soft eating cake with a rich chocolate taste, I have left the addition of an alcohol choice to you so this can reflect your favourite tipple.

INGREDIENTS

Moist chocolate cake base:
440g Self-raising flour
440g Margarine
440g Caster sugar
25g Baking powder
625g Eggs
65g Warm water
125g Cocoa powder

Dark chocolate ganache:
400g Whipping cream
100g Liquid glucose
750g Dark chocolate (70%)

Stock syrup (makes 350ml):
150g Caster sugar
300ml Water

Filling:
100g Apricot jam

Shiny chocolate sauce:
125g Milk (full cream)
50g Liquid glucose
2g Leaf gelatine
150g Dark chocolate
150g Dark cooking chocolate

Finishing:
250g Natural marzipan
Chocolate curls and spheres, as desired

METHOD

Moist chocolate cake base:

1. Using a cake mixer beat the flour, margarine, sugar and baking powder together – this will form a fine paste.
2. By hand whisk together the eggs, water and cocoa powder into a smooth paste (powder in the bowl first, adding the liquid as you whisk).
3. Add the liquids into the flour mixture, beating until smooth for approximately 3 minutes.
4. Divide the batter into two 25cm cake tins prepared and paper lined.
5. Bake in an oven preheated to 180°C for 35-40 minutes.
6. Allow the cakes to cool in the baking tins.
7. When cold store in a plastic bag or an airtight container.
8. This cake is best made the day before you need to use it.

Dark chocolate ganache:

1. Bring to the boil the cream and the glucose.
2. Pour onto the chocolate, leave for 1 minute and then stir to combine the ingredients.
3. Stir occasionally until all the chocolate is melted.
4. Leave to cool completely (better to cover with plastic to prevent skinning).
5. When cool but still soft use as below.

Stock syrup:

This will make approximately 350ml stock syrup, but any surplus can be kept in a sealed container in the fridge for up to three weeks and used to dress any type of summer fruit or salad.

1. Put the sugar and water in a small, heavy-based pan and heat gently until the sugar has dissolved.
2. Bring to the boil for 5 minutes.
3. Allow to cool, then strain and transfer to a glass container with a lid, and place in the fridge until required.
4. When adding a strong alcohol 'soak' to a sponge cake it is better to mix equal quantities of stock syrup and spirit together – this ensures the flavour does not dominate.

Assembly:

1. Take a bottom layer and spread with a very thin layer of dark chocolate – this is literally a very thin 'spreading' so it creates a firm base to the bottom of this torte. When dry, place this chocolate-side down on a 30cm cake board.
2. Spread an even layer of ganache, approximately just over one-third of the above recipe, to cover the surface.
3. Place into position the next layer of cake, sprinkle into this the alcohol soak – your choice of brandy, Grand Marnier, Cointreau or your favourite spirit mixed with an equal quantity of stock syrup.
4. Use 100g syrup/alcohol mix divided between the three cake layers.
5. After the 'soak' spread this layer with the apricot jam.
6. Place in position the next layer of chocolate cake, add the alcohol soak and then spread this over with another generous third of the ganache.
7. Place the next layer of chocolate cake in position, again sprinkle on the remaining syrup/alcohol soak.
8. With the remaining ganache thinly coat the top and sides of the torte, ensuring a smooth straight finish.
9. Place in the fridge.

Shiny chocolate sauce:

1. Bring the milk and glucose to the boil.
2. Soak the leaf gelatine in cold water until soft. Squeeze out the excess water and add to the boiled milk and glucose.
3. Melt both chocolates and add to the milk mixture.
4. Place in an airtight container and leave overnight.
5. When required warm the sauce to 35°C.
6. The sauce can be stored in an airtight container in the fridge and will keep for up to 6 months.
7. Roll out the marzipan into a circle approx 380mm diameter using a little icing sugar to prevent sticking to the table and rolling pin. This is a very thin marzipan covering to seal in the cake and add another taste dimension. Place over the ganache-coated cake, trim off any excess, using a plastic smoother to ensure a flat top and smooth straight sides.
8. Pour the warmed chocolate sauce over the marzipan using a palette knife to spread and ensure an even thin coat. 'Tapping' the board on the table also helps to ensure a smooth even coat.

9. Clean any excess sauce from around the cake board and allow to dry.
10. At this stage any chocolate decoration pieces can be added to the top, where the setting sauce will hold them in place. Illustrated are some Chocolate curls and 'marbled' spheres, see page 165 and 154.

This cake could be a delightful birthday cake for a 'chocoholic'.

Chocolate and Coffee Cake

Chocolate and Coffee Cake

SERVES 8

This recipe marries together a traditional moist chocolate cake with a more unusual water-based custard which allows the intense coffee flavour to shine through. Combine this with sticky sweet icing and you have a delicious taste sensation.

INGREDIENTS

Cake:
100g Unsalted butter
200g Caster sugar
2 Whole eggs
45g Cocoa powder
5g Baking powder
5g Bicarbonate of soda
1 pinch Salt
170g Plain flour
160g Full-fat milk

Coffee custard:
30g Golden syrup
250g Caster sugar
20g Instant coffee
300g Water
100g Cornflour
80g Water
45g Unsalted butter

Icing:
120g Icing sugar
20g Boiling water
A little instant coffee to flavour and colour

Decoration:
A few chocolate coffee beans

METHOD

Chocolate and coffee cake

1. In a mixer using a beater attachment, place the butter (at room temperature) along with the sugar. Cream together until light.
2. Add the eggs one at a time, beating well. Scrape down the bowl after each addition.
3. Sieve all the dry ingredients together, adding to the mixing bowl in two portions and mix on slow speed until the batter is clear.
4. Slowly stream in the milk.
5. Divide the mix between two greased and floured 18cm cake tins.
6. Bake at 170°C for 25 to 30 minutes.

Custard:

1. Put the golden syrup, sugar, coffee and 300g water into a pan and bring to the boil, whisking occasionally.
2. Mix the cornflour with the 80g water, whisking briskly as you add this to the boiling mixture. The consistency should be that of thick glue (add a little more water if too thick).
3. Bring back to the boil, whisking all the time. Boil for a couple of minutes to ensure the cornflour is cooked.
4. Remove from the heat and add the butter.
5. Pour into a bowl, cover with cling film and chill in the refrigerator until cold and firm.

Assembly:

1. Skin the top crust off both cakes and split each into two discs.
2. Spread approximate 30 per cent of the custard onto each layer of cake as you pile them together.
3. Use the remaining custard to mask around the sides and top to seal the cake with a very thin layer of custard.
4. Mix the icing ingredients together and pour over the top of the cake, allowing it to flow down the sides here and there.
5. To complete, sprinkle with a few chocolate coffee beans.

Chocolate Cupcakes

MAKES 24

Chocolate Cupcakes

Cupcakes have become popular for many types of celebrations – what could be better than a delicious all-chocolate one?

INGREDIENTS

Chocolate cupcakes:
340g Self-raising flour
60g Cocoa powder
400g Butter or margarine
400g Caster sugar
8 Whole eggs

Chocolate fudge filling:
450g Block fondant
30g Water
100g Icing sugar
50g Cocoa powder
30g Milk powder
100g Butter
80g Dark chocolate

Chocolate flowers:
Dark chocolate, tempered
White chocolate, tempered
Coloured chocolate

METHOD

Chocolate cupcakes:

1. All ingredients should be at room temperature.
2. Sieve together the flour and the cocoa powder twice.
3. Cream the butter or margarine.
4. Add the sugar in stages and beat well until thick and fluffy.
5. Add the eggs slowly mixing all the time.
6. Fold in the sieved flour and cocoa powder.
7. Pipe into bun cases two-thirds full.
8. Bake at 180°C for 20 to 25 minutes.
9. When baked the cupcakes should spring back when gently pressed.
10. Allow to cool on removal from the oven.
11. Using a 2.5cm plain biscuit cutter cut halfway through each cupcake, twist the cutter and remove the 'plug' of cake.
12. Pipe a bulb of chocolate fudge filling into the hole and replace the 'plug', pushing down so the top is level.
13. Temper the milk chocolate.
14. Dip the top of each filled cup cake into the chocolate.
15. Pipe a whirl of chocolate fudge filling on to the chocolate.
16. Top each whirl with a chocolate flower.

Chocolate fudge filling:

1. Soften the fondant with the water until it is workable.
2. Put the fondant, icing sugar, cocoa powder, milk powder and the butter in the bowl of an electric food mixer. Beat on the medium setting for 2 minutes.
3. Melt the chocolate and add to the other ingredients, then beat for 1 minute.
4. Scrape down the mix into the centre of the bowl and beat again for a further 4 minutes.
5. If necessary, you can adjust the consistency of the fudge icing by adding a little more icing sugar.
6. Keep in a sealed airtight container before use.

Chocolate flowers:

1. With a little practice these flowers can be piped 'free hand' but initially if you need assistance just draw a template on the back of a sheet of baking parchment.
2. Place the copied outline under a sheet of thick plastic.
3. Place tempered dark chocolate in a small greaseproof paper piping bag and snip off the end to create a small hole.
4. Pipe the outline of the petals and allow to dry.
5. Place tempered white chocolate in a small greaseproof paper piping bag and snip off the end to create a small hole.
6. Fill in each petal with white chocolate and allow to dry.
7. When the chocolate is completely set (around 20 minutes) it will easily peel from the plastic revealing a glossy shiny side.
8. Onto this side you can now pipe a 'centre' for your flowers in coloured chocolate.

Note: these flowers are extremely fragile so handle with care.

83

Chocolate Pecan Brownies

MAKES 35

An every day treat – delicious soft gooey brownies. Simple to make they are a hit time after time, this basic brownie recipe can be very versatile. For a change try substituting the pecans for your favourite nuts – walnuts, macadamias, brazil and even chopped peanuts all work well.

INGREDIENTS

200g Dark chocolate (70%)

125g Unsalted butter

225g Caster sugar

5g Vanilla paste

2 Whole eggs

1 Egg yolk

25ml Instant coffee, freshly made

135g Plain flour

5g Baking powder

1 pinch Salt

20g Cocoa powder

100g Pecan nuts, broken quite small

METHOD

1. Line a 30 x 20cm roasting pan with foil.
2. On low power melt the chocolate in a plastic bowl in the microwave.
3. Cream the butter and sugar until light, then stir in the vanilla paste
4. Add all the eggs in three portions, beating well between each addition.
5. Stir in the chocolate and the coffee.
6. Sieve the flour, baking powder, salt and cocoa powder together, then fold into the batter along with the pecans and mix through.
7. Deposit the mix onto a prepared baking tray and, using a pallet knife, spread out evenly.
8. Bake at 180°C for 20 to 25 minutes.
9. When cold cut into small squares to serve.

If you wish to make a nut-free version substitute the nuts with chocolate chips to create a 'double chocolate' brownie. Or by using a combination of white, milk and dark chocolate you can create a delicious variation on a favourite.

Centrepiece Cakes

Agni

Agni is the Hindu God of fire, an appropriate name for this centrepiece cake made from what look like delicate 'flames' of thin chocolate dancing around this elegant shape.

For cake ingredients and sizing see the quantities matrix on page 167.

EQUIPMENT

Cake boards

Marble or granite slabs that fit in your freezer

Metal scraper

Bowl

Palette knife

Illustrated here the cakes are 30cm, 23cm, 15cm and 7.5cm. Place the base cake on a 45cm cake board and the other three on boards the same sizes as the cakes.

Decide on the size of cakes and the number of tiers you are going to use, based on the number of portions required or on the impact you want your centrepiece cake to have at your reception (see the quantities matrix on page 167).

METHOD

Getting started:

1. Layer the cakes with your choice of filling; ensure they are level and straight. Coat the top and sides with a very thin spreading of filling (see page 158).
2. Cover with a very thin layer of marzipan, ensuring the marzipan covers the side of the boards the top three cakes are sat on (see page 160).
3. Check the cakes are straight, smooth and level (see page 163).
4. Stack the cakes, dowelling the bottom two tiers to ensure they take the weight (see page 164).
5. Calculate the required amount of white ganache/sauce for coating (see matrix on page 167).
6. Coat the stacked cakes when you are ready to start adding the decoration pieces and allow to start to set.

Decoration calculation:

The amount of chocolate required for the finishing techniques is a simple calculation, this obviously does vary a little depending on how thick you make the flame pieces:

There are approximately 26 pieces around the 15cm cake, each piece weighs approximately 10g, therefore it uses 260g chocolate.

- Divide 260 by 15 = 17 and then multiply by cm size of the cake
- 7.5cm requires approximately 128g
- 15cm requires approximately 260g
- 23cm requires approximately 390g
- 30cm requires 510g
- Total required for this size four tier is approximately 1.288kg.
- You need to allow approximately 25 per cent more for working (approximately 1.6kg).

Spread the chocolate for each 'flame'

Fold in the bottom of each 'flame'

Apply each 'flame' to cake

Add chocolate spheres around the cake base

Construction:

1. The slabs should be frozen.

2. Melt some of the chocolate in a bowl (this does not need to be tempered).

3. Using a palette knife take a portion of chocolate and spread it on the frozen slab, 'as if spreading butter on bread' with a 'sweeping' motion from right to left to create an arc approximately 10cm long. The chocolate will set almost immediately so slide the knife under it to release it from the slab.

4. Fold in the bottom of the 'flame' – this adds stability to the piece and makes a better surface to attach to the cake.

5. Start by wrapping two or three flames together to make a 'crown' that sits in the middle of the top cake and forms the highest point.

6. As you make each 'flame' attach it straight onto the cake so they become firm in situ. As you start attaching on the side of the top tier ensure the flame stands up 4-5cm above the edge of the cake. Work around the cake, overlapping here and there, bending the pliable chocolate into shape before it becomes brittle.

7. When you have completed a full circle start on the second row of 'flames', again overlapping by around 5cm, pinching and tweaking to create a natural appearance. A third row of the pieces will complete the first cake.

8. Continue to work down the cake. completing each tier in turn.

9. A white chocolate hollow ball is placed in a neat row to hide the final join between the last row of flames and the ganache-covered cake board.

Place the chocolate spheres around the cake base

10. The hollow balls can either be two moulded half spheres put together to form a ball or you can purchase hollow 'truffle' spheres (which are designed to be filled with ganache before rolling in chocolate as truffles) – these spheres have a small hole in one side which can be placed board-side down so it does not show.

11. The cake can be accented or complemented by the addition of a coloured ribbon glued around the cake board to add the finishing touch.

12. A sprinkle of edible sparkle dust over this cake looks super. Because the chocolate is so fine, the light reflects through and picks up the colours in the glitter, giving a very fairytale-like appearance.

Often when you first use the slab straight from the freezer it can be too cold and the chocolate will not roll because it is brittle. Disregard the first few 'spreadings' and you will soon get the required plasticity. Likewise when you can no longer lift the strips from the slab it is too warm and should be returned to the freezer to chill down again. To continue working this is where you need a second slab to alternate with.

For cake ingredients and sizing see the quantities matrix on page 167.

Andora

A simple understated stylish cake, where the accent colour of the wedding can be matched and easily incorporated.

EQUIPMENT

Dowels

Heavy-weight plastic (guitar sheets)

Palette knife

Smoother

Marble or granite slabs that fit in your freezer

Bowl

Metal scraper

Illustrated here the cakes are 30cm, 23cm, 15cm and 7.5cm (deeper cakes). Place the base cake on a 40cm cake board and the other three on boards the same sizes as the cakes.

Decide on the size of cakes and the number of tiers you are going to use, based on the number of portions required or on the impact you want your centrepiece cake to have at your reception (see the quantities matrix on page 167).

METHOD

Getting started:

Layer the cakes with your choice of filling; ensure they are level and straight. Coat the top and sides with a very thin spreading of filling (see page 158).

Cover with a very thin layer of marzipan (see page 160).

Ensure you cover the cake board edges on the top three tiers.

Check the cakes are straight, smooth and level (see page 163).

Stack the cakes, dowelling the bottom three tiers to ensure they take the weight (see page 164).

1. Calculate the required amount of white ganache/sauce for coating (see quantities matrix on page 167).
2. Coat the stacked cakes and allow to skin before you start to add the decoration.

Decoration calculation:

The amount of chocolate required will vary depending upon dimensions and the depth you choose to make. To give you a guide, for the sizes shown here it requires approximately 3kg.

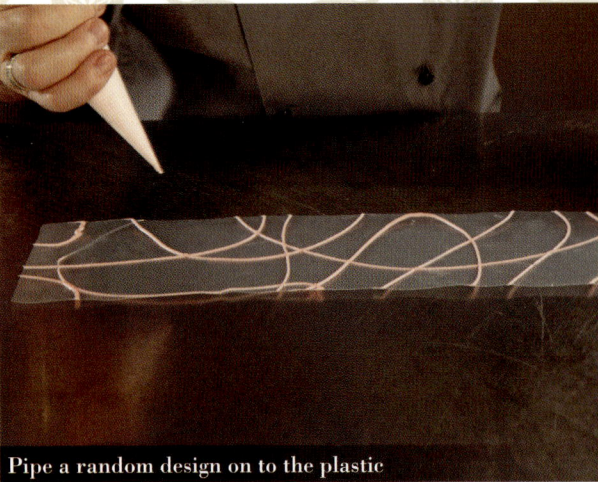
Pipe a random design on to the plastic

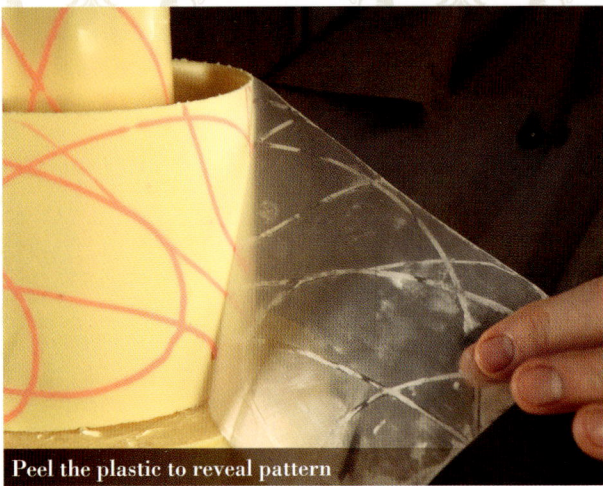
Peel the plastic to reveal pattern

'Wrap' the cake with the chocolate on plastic

Construction:

1. To create the straight clean sides for this design you need to cut pieces of heavy-weight plastic (guitar sheets) that are 30mm taller than the depth of the cakes and that overlap by 2mm when fitted around the cake.

2. Lay out the plastic on to a flat surface – the swirl pattern is made by piping with coloured tempered chocolate onto the sheet to create the desired effect. Allow to dry.

3. Using a palette knife, spread tempered chocolate onto this to an even depth of 2-3 mm; when you spread go beyond the edge of the plastic to ensure you get an even coverage.

4. While the chocolate is still liquid lift the plastic to clean the edges and lay down on a clean part of the table. The chocolate will start to 'firm up' – while it is still pliable but not liquid, lift the strip and wrap tightly around the cake. Use a smoother over the plastic to ensure a good straight smooth grip to the cake.

5. Repeat the same process for the other tiers.

6. For the larger cakes the aid of another person helps when fitting the coated plastic around the cakes.

7. Allow time for the tempered chocolate to fully harden – remember, the temperature of the work room can affect this; the ideal air temperature to work with chocolate is 18°C. The chocolate should be completely set in about 30 minutes. Gently peel the edge of the plastic then remove it from the chocolate in one smooth movement – if you don't you will create lines each time you stop.

8. Peel the plastic from each cake.

9. The base board around the cake can be coated carefully in chocolate with a palette knife – the down side of doing this is that, as you know, when tempered chocolate sets it shrinks and this can result in a crack across the chocolate which would need to be filled. The other option, which is preferable, is to make a ganache and coat the board with this (see recipe page 158).

Cut strips on a marble slab

'Pleat' the chocolate while pliable

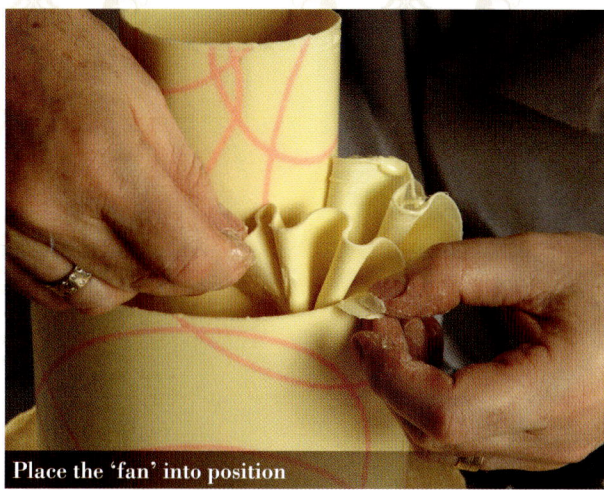
Place the 'fan' into position

'Fan' in place

To create the fan infill pieces:

1. The slabs should be frozen.

2. Melt some of the chocolate in a bowl (this does not need to be tempered). Using the metal scraper, take a portion of chocolate and spread it on the frozen slab. Spread it out into a thin even layer with a 'stroking' motion in one direction, towards you.

3. Use the corner of the scraper to slice into approximately 6-7cm wide strips.

4. Use the scraper to slide under the strips to release from the slab.

5. Pick up the strip and fold backwards and forwards to create a 'fan', then place in position on the cake while still pliable so you can tweak it into shape where required.

6. Fill in the space on the top tier and then work downwards, filling each 'ledge' around the cakes. Finish by placing a few folded fans around the cake on the coated base board in an artistic manner.

7. The cake can be accented or complemented by the addition of a coloured ribbon glued around the cake board to add the finishing touch.

Rather than more tiers I make this cake design deeper with the bottom tier just more than half as deep again than usual, the next one a little less than this, the next a little less again and the top tier normal cake depth.

Bubble

'Just call me bubbles darling ... everybody does'!
Delicious hollow spheres made in four shades of milk
chocolate, randomly stacked around a four-tier cake.

For cake ingredients and sizing see the quantities matrix on page 167.

EQUIPMENT

Dowels
Plastic bowl
Metal baking sheet
Piping bag
Freeze spray aerosol

Decide on the size of cakes and the number of tiers you are going to use, based on the number of portions required or on the impact you want your centrepiece cake to have at your reception (see quantities matrix on page 167).

Illustrated here the cakes are 30cm, 23cm, 15cm and 7.5cm. Place the base cake on a 45cm cake board and the other three on boards the same sizes as the cakes.

97

Melting the surface of the balls

METHOD

Getting started:

1. Layer the cakes with your choice of filling; ensure they are level and straight. Coat the top and sides with a very thin spreading of filling (see page 158).

2. Cover with a very thin layer of marzipan. Ensure the top three cakes which are sat on boards of the same size are coated including the board edges (see page 160).

3. Check the cakes are straight, smooth and level (see page 163).

4. Stack the cakes, dowelling the bottom three tiers to ensure they take the weight (see page 164).

5. Calculate the required amount of milk ganache/sauce for coating (see matrix on page 167).

6. Coat the stacked cakes and the base cake board altogether; allow to skin before you start to add the hollow chocolate 'bubbles'.

Decoration calculation:

1. The chocolate ball sizes I have used are 5cm, 4cm and 2cm diameter, all created in varying shades of milk chocolate (by mixing different amounts of white chocolate in with the milk chocolate).

2. Colour can be incorporated into this design by producing some coloured chocolate balls, either solid colour or marbled.

3. To make the balls see method for working with moulds see page 154.

4. To achieve the effect in the photograph and for the size of cakes in this recipe you will need approximately 5kg chocolate (plus about 25 per cent extra for working with) to make the hollow balls. In 1kg of balls you get approximately 62 x 2cm, 45 x 4cm or 30 x 5cm. Here you will need approximately 60 x 2cm, 90 x 4cm and 60 x 5cm.

Applying balls to cake

Two halves put together

Construction:

1. The balls are made in two halves and joined together, with this method: half fill a small plastic bowl with boiling water.

2. Across the top of the bowl place a metal baking sheet – the heat will warm the metal surface. Take two half spheres to be joined and place them open side down on the warm sheet, move gently in a circular motion for a few seconds.

3. Pick up the two halves and press together firmly. Wipe away any small amount of excess chocolate. Reserve the completed ball on one side and repeat the process until all the balls are assembled. To prevent marking the chocolate with fingerprints etc, it is best to wear thin gloves. either fine cotton or latex, when handling it.

4. The hollow chocolate balls can be prepared well in advance. The best way to store them is airtight, in the dark and at 18°C – remember, the balls will 'bruise' or mark if you bang them together.

5. When you are ready to assemble the balls onto the stacked cake use a piping bag filled with tempered chocolate to pipe small bulbs to fix them in place and together. Start at the bottom working around and upwards to add the different sizes to the stacked cakes. Use the larger sizes first, reserving the smaller ones for the outside. You can help the assembly process by using a freeze spray aerosol, to set the chocolate 'joints' instantly.

6. You are creating a haphazard, random looking pile of balls that you have to carefully construct to give this effect.

7. To complete, add a ribbon glued to the board edge in dark brown and into the top a voile ribbon bow in two chocolate shades with long trailing ends which finishes this cake, held in place with a little chocolate.

Fiona

A spectacular peeling cone of chocolate ribbons irregularly wrapped around a stacked cake. Natural folds and edges catch the light highlighting the delicate 'paper thin' chocolate.

For cake ingredients and sizing see the quantities matrix on page 167.

EQUIPMENT

Dowels
Metal scraper
Marble or granite slabs that fit in your freezer

Illustrated here the cakes are 30cm, 23cm, 15cm and 7.5cm. Place the base cake on a 40cm cake board and the other three on boards the same sizes as the cakes.

Decide on the size of cakes and the number of tiers you are going to use based on the number of portions required or on the impact you want your centrepiece cake to have at your reception (see quantities matrix on page 167).

METHOD

Getting started:

1. Layer the cakes with your choice of filling; ensure they are level and straight. Coat the top and sides with a very thin spreading of filling (see page 158).
2. Cover with a very thin layer of marzipan. With the top three cakes which are sat on boards of the same size also coat the board edges with marzipan (see page 160).
3. Check the cakes are straight, smooth and level (see page 163).
4. Stack the cakes, dowelling the bottom three tiers to ensure they take the weight (see page 164).
5. Calculate the required amount of white ganache/sauce for coating (see matrix on page 167).
6. Coat the stacked cakes and the base cake board altogether. Allow to skin before you start to add the decoration, which consists of strips of chocolate to create what I call a 'peeling side' effect.

Decoration calculation:

The amount of chocolate required for the finishing techniques is a simple calculation, this obviously does vary a little depending how thick you make the strips. A 15cm cake requires approximately 400g chocolate, therefore divide 400 by 15 = 27 and then multiply by cm size of the cake. If we round this to even numbers we get the following:

- 7.5cm requires 200g
- 15cm requires 400g
- 23cm requires 600g
- 30cm requires 800g
- Total required for this size three tier is 2kg
- You need to allow approximately 25 per cent more for working = 2.5kg

101

Making and applying chocolate strips to create peeling sides

Construction:

1. The slabs should be frozen.

2. Melt some of the chocolate in a bowl (this does not need to be tempered). Using the metal scraper take a portion of chocolate and spread it on the frozen slab. Spread it out into a thin even layer with a 'stroking' motion in one direction, towards you.

3. Use the corner of the scraper to slice into approximately 4cm wide strips.

4. Use the scraper to slide under the strips to release from the slab.

5. Starting at the top of the cake, fashion a cone with the first strip, sit this firmly on the middle of the 7.5cm cake. Take a second strip and wrap this around the cone spiralling downwards. Repeat the process of wrapping the strips, overlapping each other in the successive layers to create an overall cone shape effect for the completed cake. Gently press in position. While the chocolate is still pliable tweak the top edge backwards and forwards to create a soft folded look.

6. Often, when you first use the slab straight from the freezer, it can be too cold and the chocolate will not bend because it is brittle. Disregard the first few 'spreadings' and you will soon get the required plasticity. Likewise, when you can no longer lift the strips from the slab it is too warm and should be returned to the freezer to chill down again. To continue working this is where you need a second slab to alternate with.

7. A dusting of edible glitter over this cake looks particularly attractive; adding sparkle to its delicate fragility.

8. In the photograph you can see I have added some embellishment in the form of sprigs of tiny black seed pearls along with some crystal sprigs. This gives the cake decorator the opportunity to perhaps 'tie in' the cake to the rest of the wedding theme, incorporating a colour or a texture, be it diamante, crystals, tier drop pearls, small flowers or soft ribbon bows – all can work to good effect on this cake.

9. The cake can be accented or complemented by the addition of a coloured ribbon glued around the cake board to add the finishing touch.

For cake ingredients and sizing see the quantities matrix on page 167.

Georgia

A fabulous geometric 'angular' cake reviving 'run out' and 'lattice' techniques from a bygone era, creating a cake very much for now! Wonderful contrasts with the natural dark, milk and white chocolate.

EQUIPMENT

Dowels

Heavy-weight plastic (guitar sheets)

Palette knife

Smoother

Piping bag

Plastic or cellophane (butcher wrap)

Number 1.5 tube (nozzle)

Number 4 plain tube (nozzle), optional

Fine paint brush, optional

Illustrated here the cakes are square 30cm, 23cm and 15cm. Place the base cake on a 40cm board, glue this onto a 46cm cake board to create a stepped effect, and the other two cakes on boards the same size.

Decide on the size of cakes and the number of tiers you are going to use, based on the number of portions required or on the impact you want your centrepiece cake to have at your reception (see quantities matrix on page 167).

METHOD

Getting started:

1. Layer the cakes with your choice of filling; ensure they are level and straight. Coat the top and sides with a very thin spreading of filling (see page 158).
2. Cover with a very thin layer of marzipan (see page 160). On the top two cakes the marzipan should also cover the cake boards.
3. Check the cakes are straight, smooth and level (see page 163).
4. Stack the cakes, dowelling the bottom two tiers to ensure they take the weight (see page 164).
5. Calculate the required amount of sauce for coating (see matrix on page 167).

Peel the plastic from the chocolate

Assemble the cakes together with dowels

Level with liquid chocolate

Apply the flat side pieces

Construction:

1. To create the straight clean sides for this design you need to cut strips of heavy weight plastic (guitar sheets) that are 2mm taller than the depth of the cakes and the same length as each side (four per cake).

2. From the bottom work on one tier at a time.

3. Lay out the plastic pieces on to a flat surface.

4. Using a palette knife spread tempered chocolate onto each one to an even depth of 2-3 mm. When you spread go beyond the edge of the plastic to ensure you get an even coverage.

5. While the chocolate is still liquid lift the plastic strip to clean the edges and lay down on a clean part of the table.

6. The chocolate will start to 'firm up' but while it is still pliable but not liquid, lift the strip and fit tightly to the side of the cake.

7. Use a smoother over the plastic to ensure a good grip to the marzipan.

8. Repeat with all four panels.

9. Ensure the corners are clean and sharp, smoothing with a little liquid chocolate if required.

10. Repeat the same process for the other tiers.

11. Allow time for the tempered chocolate to fully harden – remember, the temperature of the work room can affect this; the ideal air temperature to work with chocolate is 18°C. The chocolate should be completely set in about 30 minutes.

12. Gently peel the edge of the plastic then remove it from the chocolate in one smooth movement – if you don't you will create lines each time you stop.

13. Infill each 'ledge' and the top with liquid tempered chocolate with a piping bag, taking care not to over fill. Smooth with a palette knife to ensure straight clean edges. Allow to set.

14. The base board around the cake can be coated carefully in chocolate with a palette knife, but the down side of doing this is that, as you know, when tempered chocolate sets it shrinks and this can result in a crack across the chocolate which would need to be filled. The other option, which is preferable, is to make a ganache and coat the board with this (see page 158).

Use the templates to make chocolate triangles

Triangle pieces:

1. The triangle decoration pieces are created in the style of traditional royal icing 'run outs', some of them with a lattice infill but using tempered chocolate which is much more instant. These can be prepared in advance and stored or just made as required.

2. There are templates to copy (see page 168) or draw your own on a piece of paper.

3. Place the drawing under a piece of plastic or cellophane (sometimes called 'butcher wrap').

4. You then need to draw outlines around the shapes using a number 1.5 tube (nozzle) in a paper piping bag, some in dark, some in milk, some in white tempered chocolate.

5. Once the outlines have dried decide which you are going to pipe with a lattice. Using the same tube pipe in one direction across the inner triangle and then across the other way to create the effect, again allow to dry.

6. Infill with a contrasting coloured chocolate around the outer triangle (as you can see in the photograph) – pipe using a paper piping bag but this time with either a number 4 plain tube (nozzle) or just a very small hole sniped off the end of the bag.

7. A fine paint brush can assist with ensuring you fill to the line evenly.

8. This technique does require a little practice to get good results.

9. Allow the pieces to set and dry. The chocolate will require at least 30 minutes to dry before it can be peeled from the plastic to reveal a bright shiny surface.

10. Tempered chocolate mirrors the surface that it dries on, therefore cellophane will give you a shinier finish than some plastics.

11. Arrange and fix the triangles on and around the cakes, securing in position with a small bulb of tempered chocolate.

12. The top arrangement is made by securing a small triangle of chocolate into the top of the cake – cut a small groove with a sharp knife and secure into this. Then add other triangles secured to each other and the cake top on both sides of the anchored pieces.

13. The cake can be accented or complemented by the addition of a coloured ribbon glued around the cake board to add the finishing touch.

Julie

For cake ingredients and sizing see the quantities matrix on page 167.

A centrepiece cake should be just that, a show piece that is the centre of attention. The combination of the smooth cake, the textured chocolate, all highlighted by the delicate shaded flowers, create just that.

EQUIPMENT

Textured plastic/heavily embossed wallpaper (which should be prepared by spraying with a thin layer of edible varnish from an aerosol and allowed to dry)

1 metre flexi curves

Weights

Knife

Aerosol freeze spray

Dowels

Rolling pin/plastic tube

Plastic/acetate

Paring knife

Illustrated here the cakes are round 30cm and 15cm. Place the base cake on a 40cm cake board and the other cake on a 20cm board.

Decide on the size of cakes you are going to use, based on the number of portions required or on the impact you want your centrepiece cake to have at your reception (see quantities matrix on page 167).

Chocolate 'S' piece showing textured pattern

METHOD

Getting started:

1. Layer the cakes with your choice of filling; ensure they are level and straight. Coat the top and sides with a very thin spreading of filling (see page 158).

2. Cover each cake with a very thin layer of marzipan (see page 160).

3. Check the cakes are straight, smooth and level (see page 163).

4. Calculate the required amount of dark ganache/sauce for coating (see matrix on page 167), coat each cake and allow to dry.

5. To make the textured chocolate components, use a piece of textured plastic made for the job or a heavily embossed wallpaper will give you a similar effect.

Use the point of a knife to mark where the dowels are to be cut

Create the petals for the water lily

6. Lay this flat onto a tray on the table. To create the desired shapes to flood with chocolate use 'flexi curves' which are 1 metre long, held in place where required with weights behind them and holding them tight onto the textured surface.

7. We are creating four pieces: A base plate which is almost a teardrop shape which should be based around the same dimension as the bottom tier.

8. An upright support around 12cm high.

9. A round 'plate' to sit on top of the support approximately 12cm diameter (a cake hoop can be used for this shape).

10. The decorative S shape to link the piece together.

11. Using tempered chocolate in a piping bag with a small hole, flood out each shape to around 10mm; tap the tray to ensure any air bubbles are expelled to the surface.

12. Allow time for the tempered chocolate to fully harden – remember, the temperature of the work room can affect this; the ideal air temperature to work with chocolate is 18°C. The chocolate should be completely set in about 30 minutes.

13. Gently peel the edge of the plastic then remove it from the chocolate in one smooth movement – if you don't you will create lines each time you stop.

Construction:

1. Starting with the base plate, mark carefully with a knife where the pieces are to be joined,

2. With the point of a knife scrape the area to roughen and create a groove to hold the upright pieces, do this also with the underside of the small disc. Pipe in a small amount of chocolate into the groove on the base plate, stand in the first upright and set in position with freeze spray, attach the other pieces carefully ensuring that the platform disc is level to hold the top cake.

3. You will need to place three or four dowels into the bottom cake to support the chocolate base plate. Hold in position with a little chocolate.

Use flexible rubber for texture

Create the 'folded' petals for the chrysanthemum

Assemble the chrysanthemum

Chocolate flowers:

Water lily:

1. In the photograph I have used dark chocolate and then when the flower is complete I have sprayed it with food colour to achieve this effect, but you can use coloured chocolate if you wish.

2. To add a curve to the petals you need to dry them over a rolling pin or plastic tube (make sure you anchor this down to the table with a bit of chocolate paste to ensure it does not roll over when the petals are drying).

3. Place a strip of plastic, acetate or greaseproof paper approximately 30cm long at the edge of the table. Using a small paring knife, dip the blade in the bowl of chocolate and scrape one side clean on the edge of the bowl. Start at one end of the strip, holding the strip in place with your index finger and thumb 5cm apart. Hold the knife chocolate side down and place it gently to touch the acetate (between your fingers) to create the petal shape. Lift up the knife a little to form a 'vacuum' with the chocolate and slide the knife off the edge of the table, this action leaves a line down the middle of the chocolate petal.

4. Move the 'holding' fingers to the next space on the acetate or greaseproof paper and repeat the petal-making process again and again to fill the strip. After 8-10 petals lift the strip from the table and place over the rolling pin and allow to set. You will need approximately 36 petals for the chrysanthemum flower (see picture).

5. Allow the petals to completely firm up – around 30 minutes at the optimum temperature of 18°C.

6. To assemble pipe a large chocolate button (4cm) onto a small piece of paper. Starting at the centre, position three petals close together, secure with a little chocolate and fix quickly in place by using the freeze spray. Working round and round the base fix the layers of petals to form the incurving flower (see picture of flower on completed cake).

Chrysanthemum:

1. Use coloured chocolate or spray afterwards to create the effect you desire. Cut small squares of acetate 7 x 7cm.

2. For this flower use a small palette knife and a small bowl of chocolate.

3. Place an acetate square at the edge of the table, dip the blade of the knife into the tempered chocolate and scrape one side of the knife clean on the bowl edge. Hold the acetate square at the top edge with your forefinger and thumb, then place the knife blade chocolate-side down onto the plastic and pull slowly backwards off the table, leaving the chocolate petal in place. Repeat this until you have done about 8 or 10.

4. The chocolate will have started to firm up on the ones first made so at this stage fold in the sides to join the petal together at its base, gradually opening at the other end (see picture of completed flower on cake).

5. To assemble make a small cone shape with moulding chocolate. Start at the top and attach the petals one by one with a little chocolate, setting in place with an aerosol freeze spray (see picture of completed flower on cake).

6. The cake can be accented or complemented by the addition of a coloured ribbon glued around the cake boards to add the finishing touch.

111

For cake ingredients and sizing see the quantities matrix on page 167.

Lola

This stunning chocolate cake looks equally good made in all white or as here using freeze-dried raspberries mixed in with the chocolate to give natural graduated shading in parts.

EQUIPMENT

Cake boards
Dowels
Marble or granite slabs that fit in your freezer
Metal scraper
Plastic bowl for chocolate

Illustrated here the cakes are 30, 23 and 15cm. Place the base cake on a 40cm cake board and the other two on boards the same sizes as the cakes.

Decide on the size of cakes and the number of tiers you are going to use, based on the number of portions required or on the impact you want your centrepiece cake to have at your reception (see quantities matrix on page 167).

METHOD

Getting started:

1. Layer the cakes with your choice of filling; ensure they are level and straight. Coat the top and sides with a very thin spreading of filling (see page 158).
2. Cover with a very thin layer of marzipan, the top two cakes cover the board edge in with the sides (see page 160).
3. Check the cakes are straight, smooth and level (see page 163).
4. Stack the cakes, dowelling the bottom two tiers to ensure they take the weight (see page 164).
5. Calculate the required amount of white ganache/sauce for coating (see matrix on page 167).
6. Coat the stacked cakes including the board for the largest cake, and allow to skin before you start to add the decoration, which consists of strips of chocolate to create what I call a 'peeling-side' effect along with rolled chocolate 'roses'.
7. The amount of chocolate required for the finishing techniques is a simple calculation, but this obviously does vary a little depending how thick you make the pieces.

- A 15cm cake requires approximately 400g chocolate:
- Divide 400 by 15 = 27 and then multiply by cm size of the cake
- 15cm requires approximately 400g
- 23cm requires approximately 600g
- 30cm requires approximately 800g
- Total required for this size three tier is approximately 1.8kg.
- You need to allow approximately 25 per cent more for working.

113

Using a scraper, scrap the chocolate from the slab

Apply the chocolate strips to the sides

Create the 'Peeling side' effect

Construction:

1. The slabs should be frozen

2. Melt some of the chocolate in a bowl (this does not need to be tempered) then, using the metal scraper, take a portion of chocolate and spread it on the frozen slab. Spread it out in to a thin even layer with a 'stroking' motion in one direction, towards you.

3. Use the corner of the scraper to slice into approximately 4cm wide strips.

4. Use the scraper to slide under the strips to release from the slab.

5. Start with the top tier side, place the strip in position just a little higher than the top edge, gently press in position and tweak the top edge backwards and forwards to create a soft, folded look. Repeat this process working around the top and then make successive layers working down to cover the cake. Tweak and fold while the chocolate is pliable so the 'peeling' effect is achieved.

6. Repeat the side decoration on the other two tiers.

Add the completed top rosette

Chocolate roses:

1. The slabs should be frozen as above.

2. Melt some of the chocolate in a bowl (this does not need to be tempered) then, using the metal scraper, take a portion of chocolate and spread it on the frozen slab. Spread it out in to a thin even layer with a 'stroking' motion in one direction, towards you.

3. Use the corner of the scraper to slice into approximately 6cm wide strips.

4. Use the scraper to slide under the strips to release from the slab.

5. With a little practice you can then roll up this strip, pinching in one end to secure and form the rose shape.

6. Place in position on the cake, gently pushing into place.

7. In the photograph you can see a large chocolate rosette to fill the top of the cake; this is made in a similar way to the 'roses' but adding extra 'petals' till you get to the desired size.

8. An alternative top to this cake is to fill the top with the 'roses' building up a small dome – this looks very effective.

9. Note – often, when you first use the slab straight from the freezer, it can be too cold and the chocolate will not roll because it is brittle. Disregard the first few 'spreadings' and you will soon get the required plasticity.

10. Likewise. when you can no longer lift the strips from the slab it is too warm and should be returned to the freezer to chill down again. To continue working this is where you need a second slab to alternate with.

11. As you can see from the photograph colour can be incorporated into this design. I have used freeze-dried raspberries, crushed and mixed in the chocolate just prior to spreading. Degrees of shading can be achieved by adding more or fewer raspberries.

12. Different colour shading can be achieved by using powder colours suitable for adding to chocolate. This way the colour theme of the wedding can be incorporated in the cake.

13. Remember, when mixing shades into white chocolate which is cream/yellow to start with, this affects the finished shade that you are trying to achieve.

14. The cake can be accented or complemented by the addition of a coloured ribbon glued around the cake board to add the finishing touch.

Olivia

The eye-catching clean lines and straight edges combined with the varying shades of chocolate works well with this modern design of circles, surprisingly sophisticated in its simplicity.

For cake ingredients and sizing see the quantities matrix on page 167.

EQUIPMENT

Dowels

Heavy-weight plastic (guitar sheets)

Palette knife

Smoother

Piping bag

Plastic or cellophane (butcher wrap)

Number 1.5 tube (nozzle)

Number 4 plain tube (nozzle), optional

Fine paint brush, optional

Sharp knife

Illustrated here the cakes are round 30cm, 23cm and 15cm, Place the base cake on a 40cm cake board and the other two on boards the same sizes as the cakes.

Decide on the size of cakes and the number of tiers you are going to use, based on the number of portions required or on the impact you want your centrepiece cake to have at your reception (see quantities matrix on page 167).

Make up of component pieces

METHOD

Getting started:

1. Layer the cakes with your choice of filling; ensure they are level and straight.
2. Coat the top and sides with a very thin spreading of filling (see page 158).
3. Cover with a very thin layer of marzipan (see page 160). On the top two cakes the marzipan should also cover the cake boards.
4. Check the cakes are straight, smooth and level (see page 163).
5. Stack the cakes, dowelling the bottom two tiers to ensure they take the weight (see page 164).

Apply a strip around the cake

Peel the plastic from the side of the cake

Fill in with chocolate around the top edge

Construction:

1. To create the straight clean sides for this design you need to cut strips of heavy-weight plastic (guitar sheets) that are 2mm taller than the depth of the cakes and which when fitted around the cake also overlap by 2mm.

2. Lay out the plastic onto a flat surface. Using a palette knife spread tempered chocolate onto this to an even depth of 2-3mm. When you spread, go beyond the edge of the plastic to ensure you get an even coverage. While the chocolate is still liquid lift the plastic strip to clean the edges and lay down on a clean part of the table. The chocolate will start to 'firm up' while it is still pliable but not liquid. Lift the strip and wrap tightly around the cake. Use a smoother over the plastic to ensure a good grip to the marzipan.

3. Repeat the same process for the other tiers.

4. Allow time for the tempered chocolate to fully harden – remember, the temperature of the work room can affect this; the ideal air temperature to work with chocolate is 18°C. The chocolate should be completely set in about 30 minutes.

5. Gently peel the edge of the plastic then remove it from the chocolate in one smooth movement – if you don't you will create lines each time you stop.

6. Infill each 'ledge' and the top with liquid tempered chocolate with a piping bag, taking care not to over fill. Smooth with a palette knife to ensure straight clean edges. Allow to set.

7. The base board around the cake can be coated carefully in chocolate with a palette knife, the down side of doing this is that, as you know, when tempered chocolate sets it shrinks and this can result in a crack across the chocolate which would need to be filled. The other option which is preferable, is to make a ganache and coat the board with this (see recipe page 158).

Secure the chocolate decorations with tempered chocolate

Circle decoration:

1. The circle decoration pieces are created in the style of traditional royal icing 'run outs' but using tempered chocolate, which is much more instant. These can be prepared in advance and stored or made as required.

2. There are templates to copy (see page 168) or draw your own on a piece of paper.

3. Place the drawing under a piece of plastic or cellophane (sometimes called 'butcher wrap').

4. You then need to drawn outlines around the shapes using a number 1.5 tube (nozzle) in a paper piping bag, some in dark, some in milk tempered chocolate.

5. Once the outlines have dried fill in between them with a contrasting coloured chocolate, as you can see in the photograph.

6. Pipe using a paper piping bag but this time with either a number 4 plain tube (nozzle) or just a very small hole snipped off the end of the bag.

7. A fine paint brush can assist with ensuring you fill to the line evenly.

8. This technique does require a little practice to get good results.

9. Allow the pieces to set and dry. The chocolate will require at least 30 minutes to dry before it can be peeled from the plastic to reveal a bright shiny surface. Tempered chocolate mirrors the surface that it dries on, therefore cellophane will give you a shinier finish than some plastics.

10. Arrange and fix the hoops, circles and spots on and around the cakes, securing in position with a small bulb of tempered chocolate.

11. The top arrangement is made by securing a small disc of chocolate into the top of the cake – cut a small groove with a sharp knife and secure into this. Then add other circles secured to each other and the cake top on both sides of the anchored disc.

12. The cake can be accented or complemented by the addition of a coloured ribbon glued around the cake board to add the finishing touch.

While I think this cake looks perfect just as it is, you may wish to incorporate colour to complement your theme for the occasion. Always think 'less is more' and I would suggest the ribbon on the board edge and just the smallest of the solid 'spots' be matched to your desired colour – this would add a sprinkle of colour from the top to the bottom.

Suzie

Suzie

Perfect for a summer party – dark rich chocolate cake, creamy white chocolate, fresh seasonal fruits served with a glass of bubbly – delicious.

For cake ingredients and sizing see the quantities matrix on page 167.

EQUIPMENT

35, 15 and 7½cm diameter boards (select sizes to suit your finished requirements)

Marble slab, frozen

Dowels

Metal scraper

Decide on the size of cakes and the number of tiers you are going to use, based on the number of portions required or on the impact you want your centrepiece cake to have at your reception (see quantities matrix on see page 167).

METHOD

Getting started:

1. Place the base cake on a board, in this case 35cm diameter and the other two cakes sit on boards the same size as the cakes.
2. The cake bases are layered with chocolate ganache (see page 158).
3. Coat each cake with a thin layer of marzipan (see page 160). With the top two cakes cover over the cake board as well.
4. Check the sides are straight and the top level (see page 163).
5. Dowel and stack the other two tiers on top (see page 164).
6. Once stacked coat the cakes and board with a layer of white chocolate sauce/ganache (see page 158).

Illustrated here we have a small round three tier made from 23, 15 and 7½cm cakes.

Spread chocolate onto a frozen slab

Make a diagonal cut across the chocolate, release from the slab

Wrap around the cake whilst still flexible

Add the fruit to the outside of the cake

Construction:

1. The 'wrapped' chocolate spiral is created by using melted white chocolate (this does not need to be tempered).

2. Take a marble or granite slab that has spent several hours in the freezer (getting the slab very cold gives you the maximum working time).

3. Using a metal scraper spread a thin smooth layer of chocolate 'massaging' backwards and forwards to get an even smooth layer – this technique requires a little practice to get the required thickness correct.

4. Using the corner of the scraper cut a straight edge along both long sides and remove the trimmings.

5. Next, make a cut across the middle of the chocolate to create two pieces that are narrower at one side than the other (by how much depends on the depth of the cakes to be covered).

6. Slide the scraper under the chocolate to release it from the slab. Working swiftly, take hold of the chocolate and form a curl at the thicker end, placing this at the back of the top tier, wrapping the chocolate around and down, take the next piece and continue to spiral around and down, overlapping as required to create the desired effect.

7. When you first take a strip of chocolate off the frozen slab it can be very cold and brittle – in this state it would not curl and bend so allow a few seconds for it to warm up in the air and then it can be manipulated.

8. Remember, because this chocolate is un-tempered and we are 'shocking' it by freezing on the slab it is very easily melted in this un-stable condition, so handle as little as possible.

9. Once the cakes have been 'wrapped' in chocolate allow time for the chocolate to become stable – a couple of hours at cool room temperature should be sufficient time to allow all to firm up.

10. While it is possible to complete this cake in a few hours, I would always do it the day before it was required, and then add the fresh fruit as close to the function time as possible.

11. A ribbon glued around the board edge to complement the fruit colours completes this cake.

Tiffany

Here is a new take on a very traditional style of cake decorating – 'run out collars' created in chocolate along with flat run out flowers and chocolate leaves collectively create a visually outstanding cake.

For cake ingredients and sizing see the quantities matrix on page 167.

EQUIPMENT

Dowels
Heavy-weight plastic (guitar sheets)
Palette knife
Smoother
Paper piping bags
Plastic/cellophane (butcher wrap)
Number 1.5 tube (nozzle)
Finer piping tube (nozzle)
Number 4 plain tube (nozzle)
Fine paint brush, optional

Illustrated here the cakes are round 30cm, 23cm, 15cm and 7.5cm. Place the base cake on a 45cm cake board and the other three on boards the same sizes as the cakes.

Decide on the size of cakes and the number of tiers you are going to use, based on the number of portions required or on the impact you want your centrepiece cake to have at your reception (see quantities matrix on see page 167).

METHOD

Getting started:

1. Layer the cakes with your choice of filling; ensure they are level and straight. Coat the top and sides with a very thin spreading of filling (see page 158).
2. Cover with a very thin layer of marzipan (see page 160). On the top three cakes the marzipan should also cover the cake boards.
3. Check the cakes are straight, smooth and level (see page 163).
4. Stack the cakes, dowelling the bottom three tiers to ensure they take the weight (see page 164).

Apply a strip of chocolate around the cake

Peel the plastic plastic from the side of cake

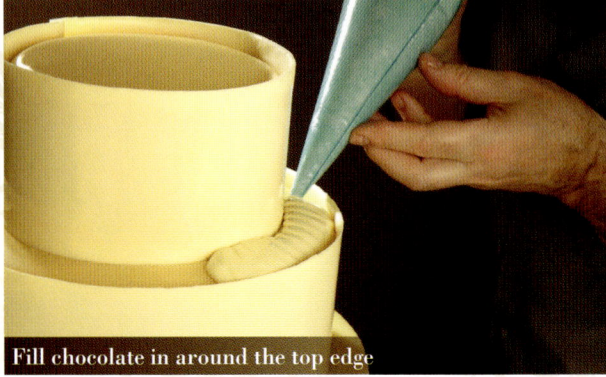
Fill chocolate in around the top edge

Construction:

1. To create the straight clean sides for this design you need to cut strips of heavy-weight plastic (guitar sheets) that are 2mm taller than the depth of the cakes and that overlap by 2mm when fitted around the cake.

2. Lay out the plastic onto a flat surface. Using a palette knife spread tempered chocolate onto this to an even depth of 2-3 mm. When you spread, go beyond the edge of the plastic to ensure you get an even coverage.

3. While the chocolate is still liquid lift the plastic strip to clean the edges and lay down on a clean part of the table. The chocolate will start to 'firm up'. While it is still pliable but not liquid, lift the strip and wrap tightly around the cake. Start with the top tier, using a smoother over the plastic to ensure a good grip to the marzipan. Repeat the same process for the other tiers.

4. Allow time for the tempered chocolate to fully harden – remember, the temperature of the work room can affect this: the ideal air temperature to work with chocolate is 18°C. The chocolate should be completely set in about 30 minutes.

5. Gently peel the edge of the plastic then remove it from the chocolate in one smooth movement – if you don't you will create lines each time you stop.

6. Infill each 'ledge' and the top cake top with liquid tempered chocolate with a piping bag, taking care not to over fill. Smooth with a palette knife to ensure straight clean edges. Allow to set.

7. The base board around the cake can be coated carefully in chocolate with a palette knife, the down side of doing this is that, as you know, when tempered chocolate sets it shrinks and this can result in a crack across the chocolate which would need to be filled. The other option, which is preferable, is to make a ganache and coat the board with this (see recipe page 158).

8. The four shaped decoration pieces for each cake are created in the style of traditional royal icing 'run outs' but using tempered chocolate which is much more instant. These can be prepared in advance and stored, or made, as required.

9. There are templates to copy (see page 168), which you may need to re-size to match the diameter of the cakes you have chosen. Alternatively create and draw your own shapes on a piece of paper.

Pipe flowers in chocolate on cellophane

Pipe curl pieces on a cake hoop or cake dummy

10. Place the drawings under a piece of plastic or cellophane (sometimes called 'butcher wrap').

11. You then need to drawn outlines around the shapes using a number 1.5 tube (nozzle) in a paper piping bag, in dark tempered chocolate.

12. Once the outlines have dried, using a finer piping tube pipe a dot (or a trio of dots) along the outside edge of each run out piece, again allow to dry and then fill in the shape with white chocolate, as you can see in the photograph. Pipe using a paper piping bag but this time with either a number 4 plain tube (nozzle) or just a very small hole sniped off the end of the bag.

13. A fine paint brush can assist with ensuring you fill to the line evenly. Allow the pieces to set and dry. This technique does require a little practice, to get good results.

14. The chocolate will require at least 30 minutes to dry before it can be peeled from the plastic to reveal a bright shiny surface.

15. Tempered chocolate mirrors the surface that it dries on, therefore cellophane will give you a shinier finish than some plastic.

16. The flowers and leaves are created in a similar way as above. You can use a template or, because they are small, do them free hand.

17. Leaves: pipe an outline in green chocolate, pipe inside this a dark chocolate shape to highlight and when dry flood over with green chocolate.

18. Flowers: pipe an outline in pink chocolate, add highlights in dark chocolate, when dry flood out in pink chocolate.

19. These pieces need to dry as above before removing from the plastic to reveal the right side with a bright shiny finish.

20. You will see on the photograph there is a piped decorative line with curls stood on top of the 'run out' pieces. This is piped on a strip of plastic with tempered dark chocolate and placed on the outside of a cake hoop, dummy or tin while it dries, giving it a curved shape. Be very careful when peeling the plastic and handling this piece as it is very fragile.

Flower decoration:

1. Peel the plastic from the run out pieces and secure in position on the cakes with small bulbs of piped white chocolate.

2. Position and secure the flowers and then the leaves into position.

3. When sticking small items to a cake with chocolate you can use an 'aerosol freeze spray' to apply a precise small blast of very cold air which instantly sets the chocolate to hold the piece in position.

4. Finally place the piped curly line decoration in place, again securing with a dot of chocolate.

5. The top 'vase' decoration is made using a plastic 'champagne saucer' which I have filled with white chocolate paste creating a dome in the top of the glass. Next secure into position some of the piped flowers and leaves with a little chocolate to complete the decoration.

6. The cake can be accented or complemented by the addition of a coloured ribbon glued around the cake board to add the finishing touch.

Zandra

Spiky and prickly by design these triangle shards of chocolate incorporate texture and patterns. Shown on the photograph here in milk chocolate it looks equally striking made in creamy white with bright coloured pattern highlights.

For cake ingredients and sizing see the quantities matrix on page 167.

EQUIPMENT

Sharp saw knife
Cake smoother
Transfer sheets
Thick plain plastic sheets (guitar sheets)
Palette knife
Ruler
Sharp knife

This cake is based on a triangle or cone shape around 50cm tall. The cake sizes I have used to construct this are 30cm, 25cm, 20cm, 15cm, 10cm and 5cm (the 10cm and 5cm cakes can be cut out of a 15cm one).

Decide on the size of cakes and the number of tiers you are going to use, based on the number of portions required or on the impact you want your centrepiece cake to have at your reception (see quantities matrix on see page 167).

METHOD

Getting started:

1. Place the base cake on a 50cm round (heavy duty) cake board. Layer and cut the cake with your desired filling (see page 158). Repeat this with each progressively smaller cake, layering them directly on top of each other and joining the cakes together (to create a cone shape).

2. When all the layers have been put together, take a sharp saw knife and, starting at the top, trim off the edges of each cake to even out the cone shape. This does not have to be precise, just take off the edges. Now coat over the entire cone shape cake with a thin layer of the filling used to layer with (eat the trimmings or use for cake pops – see page 12).

3. To cover this size cake you will need approximately 1.2kg marzipan. Roll this out into an oblong 35cm x 45cm x 5mm (approximately) thick. Lift the marzipan around the rolling pin and drape around the cake. Where the marzipan overlaps cut away the excess and 'glue' the joins together with a little water. If you need to piece the marzipan to cover completely that is fine.

4. Use a cake smoother to ensure the marzipan is firmly adhered to the cake and is as flat and smooth as possible.

5. It is better to allow this to stand overnight to allow the marzipan to firm up and skin.

6. Coat the cake and board with a layer of ganache/sauce; calculate the amount by adding what would be required for the individual cakes and halving the quantity. Allow to skin before starting to add the decoration.

Decoration calculation:

For the size of cake being created here the amount of chocolate required to make the triangle shards would be approximately 5kg plus 25 per cent in addition to allow for working.

Spread tempered chocolate onto plastic sheets

Cut out the tempered chocolate on the transfer paper

Decorate with flowers or butterflies

Mix the patterned shards with the plain shards

Construction:

1. For the shards you require two or three different transfer sheets with the patterns reflecting the colour or the theme of the celebration, also several thick sheets of plain plastic (guitar sheets).

2. With a palette knife spread tempered chocolate onto the first sheet of plastic to a thickness of about 4mm. Using the knife spread the chocolate from side to side to leave 'ripple lines' to create a textured surface.

3. As soon as the chocolate is touch dry, use a ruler and a sharp knife to cut the chocolate into 12cm wide strips and then divide these zig-zag fashion to form long thin triangles. This is only possible to do while the chocolate is still soft so you have to work with speed.

4. Repeat the above process onto the transfer sheets and again on the plain sheets to use up the 5kg chocolate (if you have excess pieces they can always be melted down and reused again).

5. Allow time for the tempered chocolate to fully harden – remember, the temperature of the work room can affect this; the ideal air temperature to work with chocolate is 18°C. The chocolate should be completely set in about 30 minutes.

6. When you handle chocolate pieces you should wear either fine cotton or latex gloves to prevent fingerprints and putting marks on the chocolate.

7. Lift and peel the triangle shards form the plastic.

8. Prepare a small bowl of tempered chocolate. Using this as 'glue', dip the short side of the triangle into the chocolate and press firmly into the cake, starting at the bottom and working around and up the cake, mixing the plain textured shards with the patterned ones to create this fabulous effect.

9. The cake can be accented or complemented by the addition of a coloured ribbon glued around the cake board to add the finishing touch.

10. Flowers, ribbons, chocolate balls or butterflies can all be used to good effect to add personalisation to this cake if required.

This is a fairly large cake and will yield approximately 100 portions. You can scale this down by using different-sized cakes to create the effect you require.

Darcy

Darcy

For cake ingredients and sizing see the quantities matrix on page 167.

These delicate rolls of chocolate give the effect of fine 'roses' completely covering each cake. I have made this design with several different accent colours, and have never been disappointed with the effect. Always looks stunning.

EQUIPMENT

Wilton 230mm long clear 'twisted legs'

White plastic 'separator plate'

Illustrated here the cakes are 30, 23 and 15cm placed on boards 10cm larger in each case.

Decide on the size of cakes, and the number of tiers you are going to use, based on the number of portions required or on the impact you want your centrepiece cake to have at your reception (see the quantities matrix on page 167).

METHOD

Getting started:

1. Place the cakes on boards then layer them with your choice of filling; ensure they are level and straight. Coat the top and sides with a very thin spreading of filling (see page 158).

2. Cover with a very thin layer of marzipan (see page 160).

3. Check the cakes are straight, smooth and level (see page 163).

4. When you are going to finish each cake coat it and the board with a layer of white ganache to act as the 'glue' to hold the 'roses' in place.

5. Calculate the amount of ganache required from the matrix on page 167, adjusting the recipe for the ganache (see page 158) to yield the correct quantity.

6. If you are creating a tiered cake this is the point at which to insert the supports, pushed right through the cakes to rest on the cake board. I am using 'Wilton' 230mm long clear 'twisted legs' with a white plastic 'separator plate' the same size as the cake  above. This type of support is very stable as the 'legs' are held firmly upright and the weight of the stacked cakes is taken between the cake boards.

7. The 'roses' that cover each cake are rolls of very thin chocolate pinched at the back to give more of a flower shape.

Place the 'roses' in position

EQUIPMENT

1-2 Granite or marble slabs that you can alternate in your freezer

Metal scraper

Bowl for the melted chocolate

Decoration calculation:

To calculate the required weight of chocolate to make the 'roses' each 'rose' weighs approximately 10g. A 15cm cake requires approx 106 'roses' (this does vary a little depending on how big you make them). I find the easiest way to work out an approximate weight of chocolate required is like this:

- To find the multiplier divide 106 by 15(cm) equals 7
- 15(cm) multiplied by 7 multiplied by 10(g) equals 1.05g
- 23(cm) multiplied by 7 multiplied by 10(g) equals 1.61kg
- 30(cm) multiplied by 7 multiplied by 10(g) equals 2.1kg
- Total chocolate for the three tiers 1050 plus 1610 plus 2.1kg equals 4.76kg

You will need to allow approx 25 per cent in addition to this to allow for working use (anything sticking to the bowl and scraper plus the trimmings from the strips can all be reused).

Spread chocolate onto a frozen slab

Make a diagonal cut across the chocolate

Release the chocolate from the slab

Make 'roses' by wrapping chocolate

Construction:

1. The slabs should be frozen

2. Melt some of the chocolate in a bowl (this does not need to be tempered) then, using the metal scraper, take a portion of chocolate and spread it on the frozen slab. Spread it out in to a thin even layer with a 'stroking' motion in one direction towards you.

3. Use the corner of the scraper to slice into approximately 6cm wide strips.

4. Use the scraper to slide under the strips to release from the slab.

5. With a little practice you can then roll up this strip, pinching in one end to secure and form the rose shape.

6. Place in position on the cake, starting with a layer all around the base and build up and around from there.

7. Note – often when you first use the slab straight from the freezer it can be too cold and the chocolate will not roll because it is brittle. Disregard the first few 'spreadings' and you will soon get the required plasticity.

8. Likewise when you can no longer lift the strips from the slab it is too warm and should be returned to the freezer to chill down again. To continue working this is where you need a second slab to alternate with.

9. As you can see from the photograph colour can be incorporated into this design. I have used freeze-dried raspberries, crushed and mixed in the chocolate just prior to spreading. Degrees of shading can be achieved by adding more or fewer raspberries.

10. Different colour shading can be achieved by using powder colours suitable for adding to chocolate. This way the colour theme of the wedding can be incorporated in the cake.

11. Remember, when mixing shades into white chocolate which is cream/yellow to start with this affects the finished shade that you are trying to achieve.

12. The cake can be accented or complemented by the addition of a coloured ribbon glued around the cake board to add the finishing touch.

Shardé

If you have ever visited the Sheikh Zayed Grand Mosque in Abu Dhabi, you will know where the inspiration for this design came from. The amazing pattern on the ceiling, which is mirrored on the carpet below, is just fabulously beautiful. I have taken elements from these designs and replicated them in chocolate to show how our creativity can be awakened by looking around us.

For cake ingredients and sizing see the quantities matrix on page 167.

EQUIPMENT

Pre-printed plastic 'transfer' sheets

Sticky tape

Knife

Palette knife

Cake smoother

Plastic/cellophane (butcher wrap)

Number 1.5 tube (nozzle)

Paper piping bag

Paint brush, optional

Illustrated here the cake is round 30cm with a depth of 25cm. Sit the cake on a 40cm round cake board which has been first covered with patterned chocolate print.

This is a one-tier extra-deep cake. Decide on the size of cake based on the number of portions required or on the impact you want your centrepiece cake to have at your reception (see quantities matrix on page 167).

METHOD

Getting started:

1. Layer the cake with your choice of filling; ensure it is level and straight. Coat the top and sides with a very thin spreading of filling (see page 158).

2. Cover with a very thin layer of marzipan (see page 160).

3. Check the cake is straight, smooth and level (see page 163).

4. The all-over pattern on this cake uses pre-printed plastic 'transfer' sheets – these sheets are available in a very wide range of pattern, colour and style. They are made by screen printing coloured cocoa butter onto the plastic; when you then coat this with tempered chocolate, allow it to set. Then, when you peel away the plastic, the pattern is left on the chocolate surface.

Construction:

1. From the patterned sheets cut out a circle the same diameter as the cake top.

2. Cut a side piece to fit exactly, butt to the top to form a straight edge.

3. If the cake is large you may find you have to join pattern sheets together which you do by securing along the length of the join with sticky tape on the opposite side to the print.

Use the stencils to draw the designs

For the board:

1. We need to put the pattern on the cake board before the cake is put in position. If the pattern is abstract as in this case and because we only require a pattern around the edge of the board, we can use strips of the transfer or 'off cuts' that we want to use up.

2. Score the cake board with the point of a knife so that when spread with chocolate, it anchors and does not 'spring away' when it sets.

3. Spread with chocolate and immediately place on the wet chocolate surface pieces of the transfer sheets print-side down and work all around the edge. Where you have an uncovered area in the middle cover this with a piece of plain plastic.

4. Place another cake board flat on top of this to ensure a smooth flat surface as the chocolate sets.

For the top:

1. I find the easiest way to tackle this is to ensure the top is level, flat and smooth.

2. Using a palette knife spread a layer of tempered chocolate over the top.

3. Immediately apply the plastic sheet, pattern-side down, ensuring that no air is trapped under the plastic as this will cause bubbles/holes in the finished surface.

4. Lay a cake board on top of the plastic to ensure a good bond is formed with the pattern and chocolate, and it's flat.

For the side:

1. Lay out the printed plastic onto a flat surface, pattern-side up.

2. Using a palette knife spread tempered chocolate onto this to an even depth of 2-3 mm. When you spread go beyond the edge of the plastic to ensure you get an even coverage.

3. While the chocolate is still liquid lift the plastic strip to clean the edges and lay down on a clean part of the table. The chocolate will start to 'firm up'. While it is still pliable but not liquid, lift the strip and wrap tightly around the cake.

4. Use a cake smoother over the plastic to ensure a good grip to the marzipan.

Release the moulded chocolate top piece

Peel the plastic from the side of the chocolate

5. Allow time for the tempered chocolate to harden fully. Remember, the temperature of the work room can affect this; the ideal air temperature to work with chocolate is 18°C. The chocolate should be completely set in about 30 minutes.

6. Gently peel the edge of the plastic then remove it from the chocolate in one smooth movement – if you don't you will create lines each time you stop.

7. The shaped decoration pieces are created in the style of traditional royal icing 'run outs' but using tempered chocolate which is much more instant. These can be prepared in advance and stored or made as required.

8. There are templates to copy (see page 168) or draw your own on a piece of paper.

9. Place the drawing under a piece of plastic or cellophane (sometimes called 'butcher wrap').

10. You then need to drawn outlines around the shapes using a number 1.5 tube (nozzle) in a paper piping bag, with tempered 'pale milk chocolate'(lighten the colour of milk chocolate with the addition of some white chocolate).

11. Once the outlines have dried pipe the pattern with tempered white chocolate within the shapes and again allow to dry. Fill in between them with milk chocolate, as you can see in the photograph.

12. A fine paint brush can assist with ensuring you fill to the line evenly.

13. Allow the pieces to set and dry.

14. This technique does require a little practice to get good results.

15. The chocolate will require at least 30 minutes to dry before it can be peeled from the plastic to reveal a bright shiny surface.

16. Tempered chocolate mirrors the surface that it dries on therefore cellophane will give you a shinier finish than some plastic.

17. The 'dome' shape is a chocolate piece cast in a mould. In the photograph this shape was made using the top of a large 'cup cake' form, but equally a large half-sphere mould could be used. Fix into position with a little chocolate.

18. The finial on the top is modelled from chocolate paste allowed to set up and then painted with edible gold colour.

19. I have added another texture to the surface by piping milk chocolate swirls over the cake board, side, top and dome.

20. Arrange and fix the shapes, securing in position with a small bulb of tempered chocolate.

21. The cake can be accented or complemented by the addition of a coloured ribbon glued around the cake board to add the finishing touch.

A GUIDE TO...

Equipment

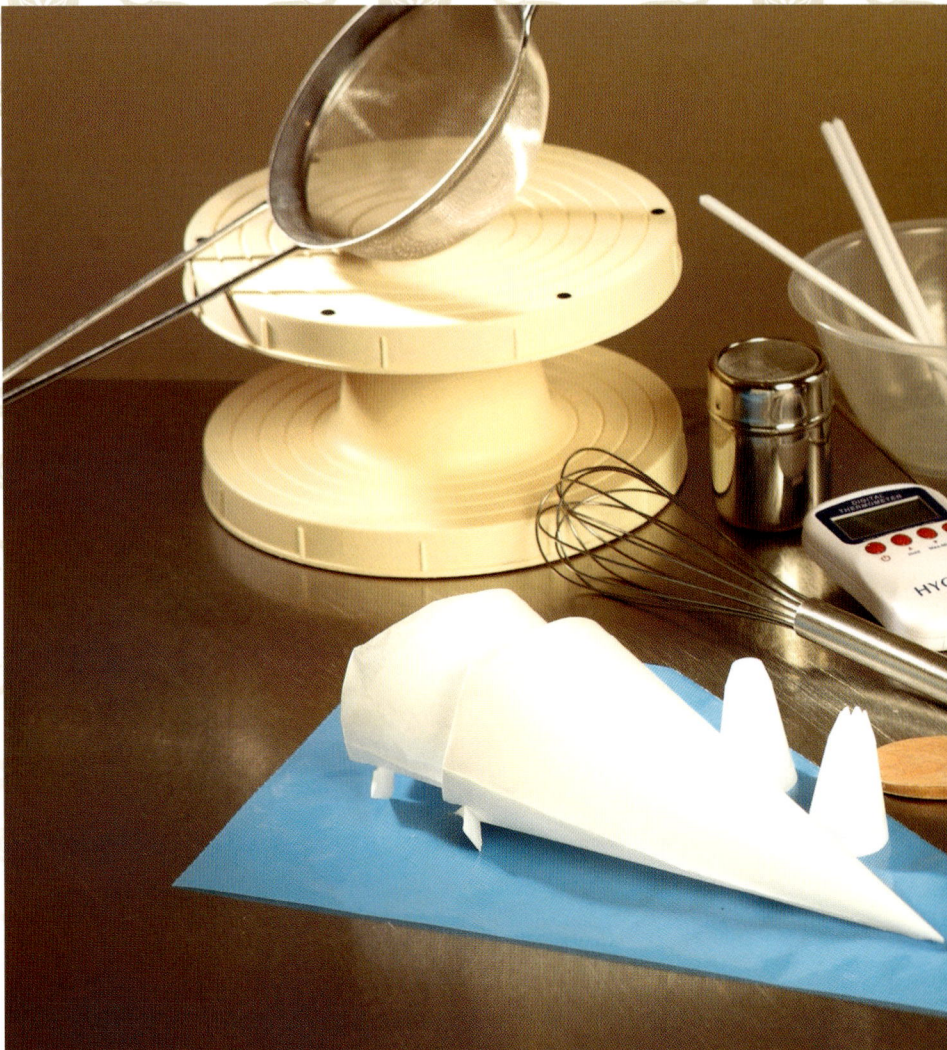

Aerograph pen - Used for spraying food colour onto cakes.

Apple corer - Can be used to remove the 'core' of cake in order to strengthen it with chocolate.

Cake dowels - Plastics rods that can be inserted into a cake to take the weight of the next tier.

Cocktail sticks - Used for marking out dowel positions on a template.

Bain-marie - Double saucepan or a pan and glass bowl combination, used for melting chocolate.

Bamboo kebab sticks - Sticks that are used for strengthening and supporting cakes and chocolate.

Cake smoother - Used for smoothing and straightening pastes after they have been applied to the cake.

Cellophane sheets - Chocolate may be spread or piped onto these sheets and easily removed once it has dried. The shiny surface of the cellophane imparts a gloss to the surface of the chocolate.

Chocolate moulds - Forms generally made from 'plexiglass' or 'macralon' that are hard plastic. These are used with tempered chocolate to create shapes that are a mirror image of the shape of the mould.

Cookie or cake cutters - Metal or plastic shapes used to cut out cake, marzipan or sugar paste.

Comb scraper - A plastic scraper with zigzag teeth, used to create patterns in chocolate, creams and icing.

Cotton gloves - Worn when handling finished chocolate pieces to prevent marking with fingerprints.

Craft knife - A very sharp, small-bladed knife used for cutting and trimming thin chocolate.

Dariole moulds - Small plant-pot-shaped moulds originally used for baking madeleine cakes, but now more commonly used as chocolate moulds.

Disposable piping bags - Triangular-shaped plastic 'savoy' piping bags, usually purchased on the roll – can be re-filled but are not washable.

Edible gold - Two types are commonly used. The first is a gold powder that is mixed with alcohol and can be painted onto chocolate with a small brush to pick out details. The second type is an aerosol that can be sprayed directly onto a cake or decoration surfaces, or applied with a brush after spraying onto a plate.

Greaseproof (wax) paper piping bags (cones) - Bags used for piping onto cakes.

Pastry brush - Small brush of food-grade quality, used for painting liquids onto solid foodstuffs.

Piping tubes (tips) - Nozzles used for piping decoration onto cakes.

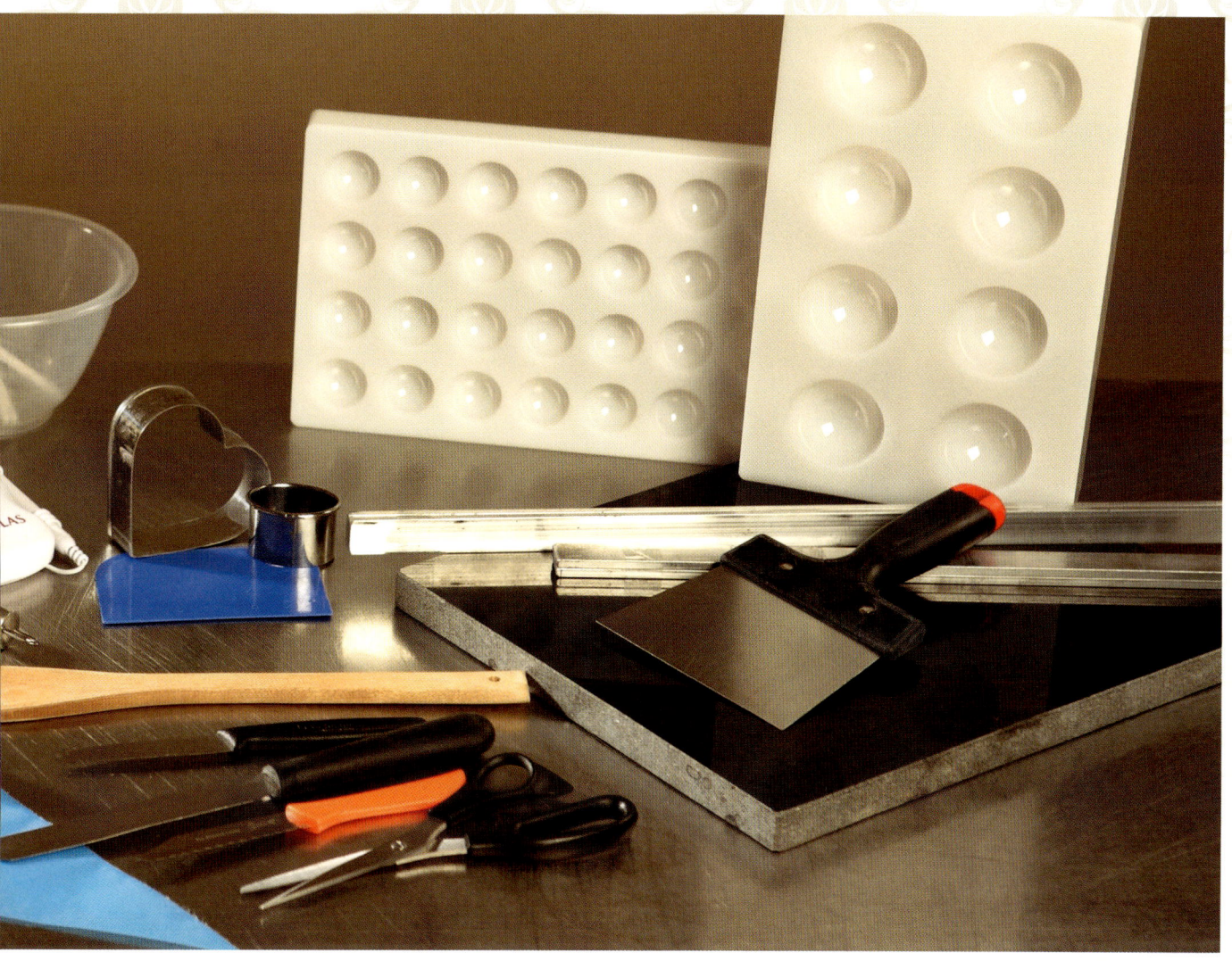

Plunger rose leaf cutter - A semi-automatic cutter that places the vein impression onto the leaf while cutting out the shape.

Rolling pin - Used for rolling marzipan and pastes and for thinning chocolate between cellophane sheets.

Savoy bag - Canvas or disposable plastic bag used for piping chocolate onto cakes.

Saw knife - A long-bladed sharp knife with a serrated edge, 25-30cm (10-12in) in length, used for cutting through a cake without ripping.

Small, sharp knife - A straight-bladed knife used for trimming and cutting pastes and marzipan.

Small sponge - Soft natural sponge used for 'dab painting' one colour of chocolate onto another.

Spacer bars - Devices that can be used for ensuring equal spacing when layering cakes.

Spirit level - Used to check that each tier of a cake is level.

Sponge roller - Used to create extremely thin and mottled chocolate coverings.

Sugar dredger - A small metal or plastic sugar shaker with a sieve or small-holed top to sprinkle icing onto the product or work surface.

Sugarpaste (rolled fondant) ribbon strip cutter - Used in sugarcraft for cutting fancy-edged strips of paste.

Thermometer - Used to monitor the temperature of chocolate.

Trowel (cranked) palette knife - A palette knife with a 'cranked' handle like a trowel.

Turntable - A cake decorator's turntable, used for the easy rotation of cakes while layering, covering and applying decorations.

Basic Techniques

Preparing cakes before you work on them is an essential part of creating and decorating chocolate cakes for celebrations. All of the centrepiece cakes in this book need to be filled and coated before they are ready to be transformed into elaborate chocolate creations and the chocolate that is used needs to be melted properly and treated correctly for successful results. Make sure that you are armed with the skills you need to achieve a stable foundation for producing truly amazing celebratory cakes.

Melting & Tempering

Working with Chocolate: Chocolate is one of the most wonderful commodities to work with. The way it looks, feels and of course, tastes is exquisite. However it is important to have a knowledge and understanding of its complexities if you are to have successful experiences working with chocolate time after time. Chocolate's only limits are your own imagination!

Tempering chocolate is an important process for a number of reasons which include the look and taste of the finished chocolate. It is the amount of crystals in the chocolate that also makes a difference and the tempering process can increase or decrease these crystals.

Pre-crystallising of the chocolate requires:

- Time
- Temperature
- Movement
- Test

These four things will help to ensure your chocolate is perfect each and every time.

Cocoa Butter:

This is dependent on the cocoa butter content and how it works within the chocolate. Cocoa butter is the fat of the cocoa bean, and it is the presence of the cocoa butter that creates chocolate with a good gloss/shine.

- Allows chocolate to release from moulds as it contracts
- Has a sensational mouth feel, melting in the mouth
- It gives the chocolate a hardness which clearly snaps when broken
- However it is the same cocoa butter that can give chocolate white streaks over its surface (fat bloom)
- It can melt very quickly when touched
- Feels grainy on the tongue (sugar bloom)
- Bends then breaks without its characteristic snap

So how is this possible?

The reasons for this very special ingredient behaving so very differently is because it is polymorphic, which means it can change depending on its circumstances at the time.

Chocolatiers now know that it's not just about the temperature of the chocolate that matters, it's about the crystal formation at the time of preparation and manufacture. Cocoa butter is thought to contain six different crystals and it can change from one to another depending on varying amounts of time, temperature and movement, given to the chocolate.

Unfortunately not all of these six crystals of a stable structure and don't lock together when set. Only stable crystals will ensure all the good qualities of chocolate.

As we can't see them, it was thought that these crystals in body temperature chocolate were stable and would give the correct formation when set. However we now know that if chocolate does not receive any or only a little movement when being melted there would be insufficient crystals present to allow the characteristics of the cocoa butter to be realised – meaning no snap, grainy etc.

EQUIPMENT:

Plastic mixing bowl

Spoon

Heat source (Bain Marie or Microwave)

Melting Chocolate:

Melting Chocolate: Good quality chocolate contains cocoa butter, and melts at a temperature just below our own body temperature.

It is therefore important not to over heat chocolate as it will burn easily. Remember, if chocolate melts at body temperature, there is no need to place it over direct heat to melt it. Chocolate melts easily if placed into an electric hot water Bain Marie, or in the low dry heat of a microwave.

Melting Tip:

The methods given to pre-crystalised chocolate are the same for white, milk and dark varieties. However due to additional milk and sugar content of milk and white chocolate extra care is needed during the melting process to ensure the chocolate does not burn and therefore become grainy and unusable.

Pre-crystallising Chocolate

EQUIPMENT:

Plastic mixing bowl

Spoon

Heat source (Bain Marie or Microwave)

Marble work top

Scraper

Step pallet knife

Pre-crystallising Tip:

Chocolate can be pre-crystallised in many ways. Choose the way that suits you. As long as the principles of creating stable crystals are adhered to its what ever works for you. You can melt chocolate over warm water – take care not to get water into the chocolate. Even in the form of steam/vapour coming from the pan as this moisture will thicken the chocolate making it difficult to work with. If you want to work using this method, wrap a tea towel around the base of the bowl with the chocolate in it to prevent vapour rising from the pan.

Table method:

Completely melt the chocolate in the microwave or electric Bain Marie. The chocolate will look very fluid, and will therefore have no crystals within it. Used in this condition all the products will be of poor quality and display all the characteristics mentioned on page 150.

Stable crystals now have to be produced, this is quite simple as we have already given the chocolate time and temperature to melt it. We now have to move the chocolate to create the stable crystals. Only a relatively small proportion of crystals are required, so pour approximate two-thirds of the liquid chocolate on a clean dry surface such as marble, granite or stainless steel. Working the chocolate backwards and forward, as it thickens the stable crystals are formed.

Before it sets, place this chocolate back into the warmer chocolate and stir well. The warmer chocolate will help bring a nice fluidity back to the chocolate and the worked chocolate and the worked chocolate will have enough stable crystals to give some to the unworked chocolate. Then when mixed back together the chocolate can be tested to make sure it has stable crystals within it will produce good quality products.

Seeding Method:

The seeding method is very similar to the table method in that the chocolate is fully melted. However instead of pouring the chocolate on the table chocolate pieces/buttons can be stirred into the warm chocolate. As all the chocolate has to pre-crystallise in order to make it set with the correct structure it makes sense to add some of this to seed the warm, liquid chocolate. This is less messy as it can be done in a Bain Marie or if using machinery in a wheel machine. The amount of pieces/buttons will depend on the type of chocolate and how much the chocolate is moved. Test the chocolate in the same way as in the table method.

Microwave Method:

The microwave method is the fastest way to pre-crystallise your chocolate and very inexpensive. Depending on the size of the bowl with the chocolate in place into the microwave for 1 minute if a large bowl, 30 seconds if small. Place on full power (up to 1000W) and then remove from the microwave.

Stir and if two-thirds of the chocolate pieces have not melted then proceed with another minute. Be flexible, it may be nearly there and only need another 30 seconds or even 10 seconds – it is important that there are some buttons remaining for this method to work.

Once two-thirds of the chocolate has melted use a heat gun or hairdryer to help the remaining buttons melt. These will seed the liquid chocolate and when all the buttons have disappeared do the following test to ensure you have a stable structure to your chocolate.

Testing the Chocolate

EQUIPMENT:

Scraper, step-pallet knife or knife

Clock/timer

Testing Tip:

Chocolatiers are often told to take a sample or test and wait 3 minutes. This is ok but in our opinion from a teaching point, it is better for the chocolate to be a little more fluid when you are learning as this gives you more time when processing the chocolate into moulds but still retains the correct amount of crystals, to give good results.

The all important test:

The test is the most important thing you can do when determining if chocolate is ready. As this will tell you before you start using the chocolate how your products will look.

Simply dip the scraper or palate knife part-way into the chocolate, scrape one side clean on the bowl edge and leave for 5 minutes. The chocolate in the bowl will be completely fine for this 5 minute period.

Chocolate has three stages in its process

1. Chocolate will be fluid – melted
2. Chocolate becomes touch dry when left to dry
3. Chocolate contracts, and it is completely dry

If the sample chocolate is touch dry in the 5 minute period your chocolate has the correct amount of crystals to ensure you will have the perfect chocolate.

However if the chocolate is still fluid after 5 minutes, you will have some stable crystals but not enough to give the chocolate a good gloss and snap when eaten.

To combat this you can either pour a little on the table and move the chocolate to create some extra crystals or add some more buttons to the liquid chocolate. Either way will increase the amount of crystals. Redo the test to check.

However the opposite can occur and the chocolate sets too quickly, all this means is you have good stable crystals but too many. Having too many might sound like a good thing but it will make the chocolate thick and very hard to work with. In this case all that is required is a little heat from the heat gun or hair dryer to reduce the amount of crystals, then redo the test.

It's important to note that as with all methods of pre-crystallising, chocolate has to remain in a good crystalline form throughout the manufacture of your items. When using the heat gun or hair dryer on chocolate which has no thermostat to control the heat, it is important to take great care. It's also worth remembering that while working with the chocolate you are creating movement which is one of the factors needed to create stable crystals. Therefore it's quite possible for the chocolate to become thick while working with it. This is easily solved by using the heat gun/hair dryer again. Little and often to keep the chocolate at its optimum crystalline state.

Using Moulds

Use moulds to create multiple interesting chocolate shapes. They are easy to use and can add wonderful detail to themed cakes. The temperature of your mould should be close to that of tempered (see pages 150-153) chocolate you are using. When creating shapes in batches, always ensure that moulds that have been refrigerated are warmed before re-use.

Solid shapes:

1. For solid chocolate shapes, simply pipe in the right amount of tempered chocolate to fill the mould completely.

2. Tap the mould onto the work surface to release any bubbles and refrigerate for about 20 minutes. (When you turn over the mould to release the shapes, the chocolate should be opaque and will have contracted, freeing itself from the sides of the mould.)

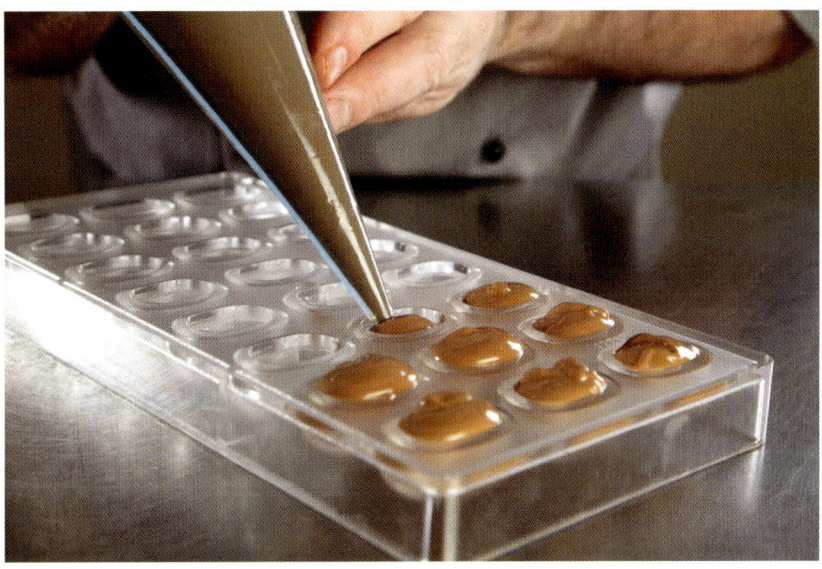

MOULD TIPS

Make sure that you keep your moulds scrupulously clean. Wash them thoroughly after use, using hand hot, water, then rinse. Dry and polish them, using soft tissue or a soft cloth. Touching the interior of moulds by hand can cause blemishes and sticking. Avoid the use of sharp metal objects, such as knives, for removing chocolate remnants, as these can damage the moulds very easily. It is preferable to use wooden spatulas or scrapers instead.

Hollow shapes:

1. Fill the mould to the brim with tempered chocolate and tap it onto your work surface to release any air bubbles.

2. Invert the mould so that the chocolate drains back into the pan, leaving a thin coating of chocolate on the sides of the mould. You can vary the thickness of the chocolate by leaving it to dry and then recoating as many times as you like.

You can add colour to moulds by brushing a contrasting-coloured chocolate into the mould and allowing it to dry before you fill it with your main chocolate. Use white chocolate tinted with powdered food colouring to create a shade that will match the wedding or celebration cake.

Base Cakes

Chocolate Cake Recipe:

I have included here two recipes – my recommended is **The Very Good Chocolate Cake** which makes a moist, good eating, dark crumb chocolate cake that cuts and layers well. It can be used as the base for all of the centrepiece style cakes. I find this cake bakes better as a thinner cake that we can cut two layers from with four layers making a 'normal' depth cake. You will see on the recipe that I split the batter into two tins to facilitate this.

The other recipe is an 'all in' **Mud Cake** style cake that seems to have become popular at the moment – this is a much more moist style of cake, to me almost a pudding texture.

A good alternative …

There are a number of good chocolate cake pre-mixes available and indeed we use one within our business that makes an excellent eating product with fine crumb texture that makes it ideal for layering and is a simple fail-safe recipe time and time again. This 'Devil's Food Cake' mix is available from our website www.slattery.co.uk (see the Quantities Matrix on page 167 for a range of sizes).

INGREDIENTS

220g Butter

220g Dark chocolate, chopped

25g Coffee granules

160g Water

200g Eggs

100g Skimmed milk

25g Vegetable oil

125g Self-raising flour

125g Plain flour

50g Cocoa powder

5g Bicarbonate of soda

480g Caster sugar

Chocolate Mud Cake:

Makes one 22cm round cake

METHOD

1. Put the butter, chocolate and coffee with the water in a plastic bowl, then heat in the microwave until it is all melted – use short bursts for a few seconds and stir regularly. Combine this with the eggs, milk and oil.

2. Sieve together the flours, cocoa powder and bicarbonate of soda into a large mixing bowl, then stir in the sugar. Create a well in the centre and add the combined liquid ingredients, stirring with a wooden spatula until completely combined and smooth.

3. Preheat the oven to 160°C. Grease the cake tin and line with greaseproof or silicone paper with a base and a collar that extends a little above the top of the tin.

4. Pour the mixture into the tin and bake for 1 hour 40 minutes or until a skewer pushed into the centre comes out clean. Leave in the tin until cold.

5. Keep in an airtight container or tin for up to 2 weeks or it can be frozen.

INGREDIENTS

350g Self-raising flour
350g Margarine
350g Caster sugar
20g Baking powder
500g Eggs
50g Warm water
100g Cocoa powder

The Very Good Chocolate Cake:

The recipe below makes two shallow 20cm round cakes, from which we can cut four layers (two from each cake) to make one cake. The sizing matrix below can be used to change the size of the cake.

METHOD

1. Using a cake mixer beat the flour, margarine, sugar and baking powder together – this will form a fine paste.

2. By hand whisk together the eggs, water and cocoa powder into a smooth paste (powder in the bowl first, adding the liquid as you whisk).

3. Add the liquids into the flour mixture, beating until smooth for approximately 3 minutes.

4. Divide the batter into two 20cm cake tins prepared and paper lined.

5. Bake in an oven preheated to 180°C for 35-40 minutes.

6. Allow the cakes to cool in the baking tins.

7. When cold store in a plastic bag or an airtight container.

8. This cake is best made the day before you need to use it.

The Very Good Chocolate Cake Sizing Matrix:

Below I have worked out the weights of the ingredients required for individual recipes to make the weight of cake batter for cake sizes from 7.5cm up to 38cm. This should help you calculate what you need when making tiered cakes (because ingredients vary this will not be 100 per cent accurate but will be a good guide).

	7.5cm / 3" cake	10cm / 4" cake	12.5cm / 5" cake	15cm / 6" cake	17.5cm / 7" cake	20cm / 8" cake	23cm / 9" cake	25.5cm / 10" cake	28cm / 11" cake	30.5cm / 12"	33cm / 13" cake	35.5cm / 14" cake	38cm / 15" cake
Self-raising flour	88g	130g	155g	198g	262g	350g	395g	440g	480g	525g	590g	615g	655g
Margarine	88g	130g	155g	198g	262g	350g	395g	440g	480g	525g	590g	615g	665g
Caster sugar	88g	130g	155g	198g	262g	350g	395g	440g	480g	525g	590g	615g	665g
Baking powder	5g	7g	9g	12g	15g	20g	23g	25g	30g	30g	35g	35g	38g
Eggs	125g	185g	218g	283g	375g	500g	565g	625g	690g	750g	815g	875g	935g
Warm water	13g	20g	25g	30g	38g	50g	60g	65g	65g	75g	80g	85g	95g
Cocoa powder	25g	35g	45g	58g	75g	100g	115g	125g	140g	150g	165g	175g	185g
Total batter weight to be split between two tins	432g	637g	762g	977g	1289g	1720g	1948	2160	2365	2580	2865	3015	3218
Batter weight per tin	216g	318g	381g	488g	644g	860g	974g	1080	1182	1290	1432	1507	1609

Ganache for Pouring or Filling

INGREDIENTS

	Dark Chocolate 54%	Milk chocolate 33%	White chocolate 26%
Whipping Cream	125g	125g	125g
Glucose	30g	30g	30g
Chocolate	175g	250g	300g
Total Weight	330g	405g	455g

METHOD

1. Bring to the boil the cream and glucose and pour over the chocolate buttons/pieces. Wait a few moments to allow the heat of the cream to warm through the buttons/pieces. Stir well to create a smooth emulsion. As the ganache cools it will become thicker – pour over the cake while still warm and runny but not hot.

2. Alternatively you can heat the cream and glucose and mix with melted tempered chocolate. Stir well and pour over the cake when the correct viscosity is reached.

3. If you wish to use this recipe for the filling in a cake, seal in an airtight container and allow to stand at room temperature overnight. When you wish to use the ganache, put it in a machine bowl with a beater and mix on medium speed until a lighter consistency suitable for spreading is achieved.

Chocolate Paste

INGREDIENTS

Syrup:
80g Water
120g Icing sugar
300g Glucose

Paste:
1kg White chocolate, tempered
500g Syrup, at 30°C

METHOD

Syrup:

Bring the ingredients to the boil then allow to cool. Use at to 30°C.

Paste:

Stir all the ingredients together and spread onto a plastic sheet, cover with a further plastic sheet and allow to set. Knead before use.

Note: The above recipe is to make white chocolate paste using white chocolate.

For dark chocolate paste add 100g tempered cocoa butter. For milk chocolate paste add 50g tempered cocoa butter.

Shiny Chocolate Sauce

INGREDIENTS

250g Whole milk
100g Glucose
4g Leaf gelatine
300g Couverture chocolate
300g Cooking chocolate

METHOD

1. Bring the milk and glucose to the boil.

2. Soak the gelatine in cold water until soft, squeeze out the excess water and add to the boiled milk and glucose.

3. Melt both chocolates and add to the milk.

4. Place in an airtight container and leave overnight.

5. When required warm the sauce to 35ºC.

6. Pour over the cake and allow to set before decorating.

7. This sauce can be stored in the fridge in an airtight container and will keep for up to 6 months

8. White, milk or dark chocolate can be used.

Chocolate Fudge Filling

This is used as an alternative to ganache for filling and coating cakes and is used in cakes. It will keep for about three months in an airtight container – it does not need to be refrigerated.

INGREDIENTS

450g Block fondant
30ml Water
100g Icing (confectioner's) sugar, plus a little extra if required
30g Cocoa powder
30g Milk powder
100g White vegetable fat
75g Dark chocolate

1. Soften the fondant with the water, so that it is workable.

2. Put the fondant, the icing (confectioner's) sugar, the cocoa powder, the milk powder and the vegetable fat into an electric mixer. Beat on a medium setting for two minutes.

3. Melt the chocolate and add it to the other ingredients. Scrape down the sides of the bowl, so that all the ingredients are in the centre, before beating thoroughly for a further 4 minutes.

4. If necessary, you can adjust the consistency of the fudge icing by adding a little more icing sugar.

5. Wrap the icing in a plastic bag to keep completely airtight before storing.

TIPS BEFORE YOU START

It is easier to cut a cake that is 24 hours old than a fresh one, so bake the required cakes one day in advance if possible.

A chilled cake is much easier to cut than a cake at room temperature, so place cakes in plastic bags (to prevent them drying out) in the refrigerator for a few hours before slicing.

Always remove the 'skin' (the outer top crust) from a cake. This will generally work loose naturally. If the skin is left on the cake while it is layered, it will bond with the coating cream and create instability in the layers.

Using a turntable makes cake manipulation much easier.

For help with cutting straight, evenly spaced slices through a cake, use spacer bars at the required thickness, to guide the knife blade.

Always use a sharp saw-type knife to cut slices through a cake. This type of knife gives a clean cut with few crumbs.

Ganache and cream are easier to spread if they are at room temperature -15°C – and have been beaten to a smooth consistency (by hand or with a machine). This also prevents the cream from pulling up crumbs from the cake surface.

Layering

Layering a cake is the process of slicing it into horizontal sections and sandwiching it with filling – usually ganache. If this basic process is completed correctly, the more creative and artistic steps that follow are much easier.

In this book, cake bases of different thickness are required. As a general rule, the final depth of a cake base (cake plus filling) should be two-thirds cake to one-third filling. Round, square and shaped bases are layered in the same way.

Slice chocolate bases into even thickness layers using a sharp serrated-edged knife

Spread the filling to an even thickness, spreading from the centre outwards

Alternate with layers of cake and filling to the required cake height

Thinly coat the top and sides of the cake; rotating the turntable helps to achieve an even coat

INGREDIENTS

Chocolate cake(s) (see pages 156)

Ganache (see pages 158) or other filling.

EQUIPMENT

Plastic bags (one per cake)

Sharp saw knife

Spacer bars (optional)

Cake board

Turntable

Palette knife

METHOD

1. Remove the cake from its plastic bag and, using a sharp saw knife, take off the skin on top of the cake.

2. Slice even layers horizontally through the cake bases, use spacer bars if required to cut even layers.

3. Often two bases (or more) are used to create one deeper cake. Place the first layer onto a cake board, then onto a turntable ready for filling.

4. Slice into layers (about 3-4) horizontally through the cake, using spacer bars if required, and place the base layer of cake onto a cake board, then onto a turntable ready for filling.

5. Put some filling on the centre of the base cake layer and spread it out into a flat, even layer, right up to the cake edge, using a palette knife.

6. Place the next layer of cake on top and repeat the layering of filling and cake until you reach the required depth.

7. Apply a thin coating of filling to the top and sides of the cakes. This stops the cake drying out and acts as 'glue' for the marzipan or paste chocolate (see pages 158).

Covering with Marzipan

Applying a layer of marzipan to a cake gives it stability and creates a barrier between cake and decoration. This also provides a firm, smooth surface that is easy to work with. If you do not like marzipan, however, you can use chocolate paste (see page 158), or you can omit the process entirely. In this case, though, it is vitally important that the underlying coat of ganache is very smooth (see page 162).

INGREDIENTS

Layered cake (see page 160)

Marzipan (or chocolate paste)

Icing (confectioner's) sugar for dusting

EQUIPMENT

Rolling pin

Cake smoother

Small, sharp knife

1. Use a rolling pin to roll out a piece of marzipan, large enough to cover the top and sides of the cake (and its cake board edge, if specified), with a small margin for trimming. The marzipan should be quite thin, but not so thin that it loses it stability. Use a little icing (confectioner's) sugar to prevent the marzipan from sticking to the rolling pin or work surface.

2. Drape the thin piece of marzipan carefully over the cake, (wrapping the marzipan around the rolling pin before you lift it may be helpful – then you can unroll it smoothly and gradually over the cake without stretching it).

3. Starting at the top centre, use a cake smoother to flatten the marzipan over the cake neatly. Use a circular motion with the cake smoother and press the marzipan into position, eliminating any air that may be trapped beneath.

4. Smooth the top of the cake, then work down the sides, ensuring a smooth, creaseless coating. Trim off any excess marzipan from around the base of the cake using a small, sharp knife. Run the smoother around the cake again to make sure that the sides are completely straight and even before you continue to work on the cake.

Levelling

When you have covered a cake, you must ensure that the surface is perfectly level; this is especially important with stacked or tiered cakes as nothing looks worse or is more unstable than a *leaning* cake.

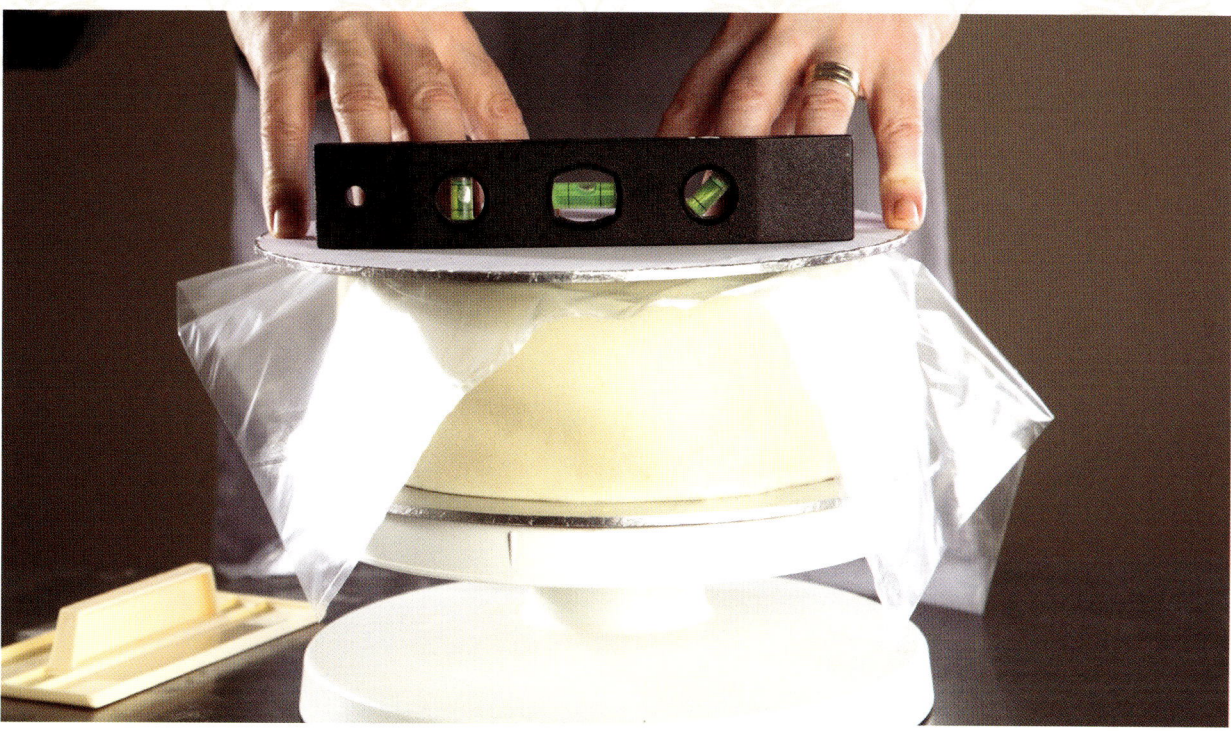

EQUIPMENT

Cellophane
Cake board
Spirit level
Weight

1. Lay a sheet of cellophane on top of the cake and put a cake board on top of this. Put the spirit level in position and apply pressure to the board to level it, if required.

2. Put a weight in position and leave the cake to stand overnight. Then, remove the cellophane and allow the marzipan to dry.

Dowelling

When making tiered cakes, as many are in this book, it is important to dowel the cakes. This means using plastic rods to support and evenly distribute the weight of the cake above, between the cake boards, so no weight rests on the cakes themselves. This creates a stable structure that can then be decorated. Please check the recipe for specific information.

Cut out paper templates of the bottom and middle cake sizes. Mark the position of the dowels on the templates by folding the circles in half, then half again. While folded, measure the centre point on both straight sides and mark firmly with a pencil so that, when unfolded, four equally spaced dots are marked. Place the template on the cake. Prick through each template to mark the dowel positions with a cocktail stick (toothpick).

Remove the templates and insert the dowels into the cakes at these points. Mark the dowels where they meet the surface of the cake, then pull them out and cut them off at this mark. Re-insert the dowels, then place the cakes on top of each other. There is no need to secure these together as the chocolate coating will hold them in place perfectly.

Textures and Curls

The flexibility of chocolate means that it can be used to create a variety of edible decorative pieces that both look stylish and taste good. Melted chocolate can be manipulated into a range of unusual shapes, adding interest to any cake. Over half of the cakes in this book contain some form of chocolate decoration that is made separately from the main cake, then placed into position. You can use different colours of chocolate as a means of creating the effect of your choice – experiment!

You can choose from curls – caramel, candy-striped, coloured or brushed with gold; short curls, loose like pencil shavings, spiralling or scraped or grated from a block of chocolate; ruffles; flat piped pieces – snowflakes and stars; textured curved shapes created on plastics and paper; hollow spheres – both solid and filigree; mottled chocolate shaped in moulds; cut shapes using a knife and templates; lattice domes; roses; draped chocolate to look like soft fabric and flat sheets of chocolate.

The possibility of using these decorations is not limited to the cakes with which they are shown in this book. Many of them would make fabulous adornments for simple desserts and puddings – particularly ice creams and bombes. Your dinner parties will never be the same again.

Glossary

Aerosol Varnish
An aerosol product offering the ability to give a thin coat of edible varnish over chocolate and marzipan products.

Cake Dowels
A solid cylindrical plastic rod used when stacking tiered cakes to take the weight between the cake boards. Can easily be cut to length with a sharp knife.

Edible Gold Paint
The gold often used on chocolate and confectionery products is a 'lustre' powder which when mixed with alcohol can be applied with a brush. There are also aerosol sprays available in gold, silver or bronze.

Flexi Curve
A flexible 'rule' that is designed to be used as a drawing aid – it can be bent and holds its shape so can be utilised to create 'fluid' chocolate outlines.

Fondant
Solid 'block' fondant is a product that can be purchased. In its simplest form it is made from sugar and water boiled to the soft ball stage and then stirred to create a thick white icing. It can be warmed and used as the icing on cakes or pastries. It can also be used as a filling in chocolates such as peppermint creams or as an ingredient in, say, buttercream.

Food Colours for Chocolate
These are fat soluble pigments that are made to be added straight into liquid chocolate. Usually in powder form but can be found as an oil-based liquid.

Freeze Spray
An aerosol product which is 'a blast of cold air in a can', used for instant set and hold when placing chocolate pieces onto a cake.

Guitar Sheets
Heavy-gauge plastic sheets onto which chocolate can be piped or spread – they can be reused several times.

Liquid Glucose
Or glucose syrup – in the USA it is known as 'corn syrup'. Commonly made from maize starch but can also be derived from potatoes, wheat, barley or rice. Glucose syrup is used in foods to soften texture, add volume, retain moisture, prevent crystallisation of sugar and enhance flavour.

Plastic Champagne Glasses
A 'saucer' style champagne glass in plastic (see suppliers for source).

Separator Plate with Twisted Legs
'Wilton' product giving a way of stacking tiered cakes with clear plastic 'legs' which go through the cake and rest on the board – these are then held in place firmly by a plate that clips into position on the top of the legs onto which the next cake sits, thus creating a very stable structure.

Textured Plastic Sheets
Acrylic sheets embossed with a wide range of patterns that can create a textured finish onto chocolate set on them. They are re-usable and are a novel way to add pattern and shape.

Toffoc Vodka
Toffoc is a trade name for the most delicious blend of toffee with vodka. It's not too sweet, it's not too sticky and it has a crystal clear golden colour.

Transfer Sheets
A plastic sheet onto which coloured cocoa butter has been screen printed, allowing us to create fantastic and colourful designs on chocolate.

Quantities Matrix

The chart below is to be used as a guide only, it will give you an idea of the quantities to be used. As we sometimes require differences in the cakes we create, more filling or less filling, deeper cake, or thinner marzipan, bigger slices or smaller portions etc then you will need to use your judgement and adjust the amounts accordingly.

Cake Size	Cake batter weight Split equally into 2 tins	Devil's food Cake Pre-mix split into 2 tins	Approx number of portions	Ganache or chocolate fudge for filling	Marzipan weight for an approx 5mm thick coat	Coating sauce or ganache	Guide weight for chocolate decoration depending on the design and style of the cake		
7.5cm / 3"	432g	360g	4	200g	150g	75g	120g	to	400g
10cm / 4"	637g	550g	7	300g	250g	100g	160g	to	600g
12.5cm / 5"	762g	700g	10	400g	375g	125g	200g	to	800g
15cm / 6"	977g	880g	15	450g	500g	150g	250g	to	1000g
17.5cm / 7"	1289g	1200g	20	530g	750g	175g	300g	to	1200g
20cm / 8"	1720g	1400g	25	600g	875g	200g	340g	to	1400g
23cm / 9"	1948g	1800g	36	680g	1000g	225g	380g	to	1500g
25.5cm / 10"	2160g	1965g	50	760g	1250g	250g	420g	to	1600g
28cm / 11"	2365g	2100g	65	830g	1400g	275g	470g	to	1900g
30.5cm / 12"	2580g	2300g	80	910g	1550g	300g	510g	to	2100g
33cm / 13"	2865g	2500g	100	1000g	1750g	325g	550g	to	2255g
35.5cm / 14"	3015g	2800g	120	1100g	1950g	350g	600g	to	2450g
38cm / 15"	3218g	3000g	145	1200g	2250g	375g	650g	to	2600g

GEORGIA TRIANGLE TEMPLATES

TIFFANY TEMPLATES

TIFFANY FLOWER TEMPLATES

SHARDE TEMPLATES

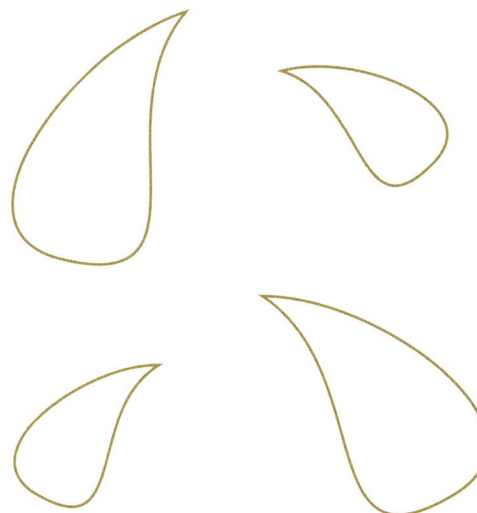

Suppliers

Most products and ingredients used in the pages of this book can be sourced from the companies listed below.

Our website www.slattery.co.uk has an online shop facility where chocolate, ingredients, moulds and many items of equipment are available.

Our unique premises on Bury New Road in Whitefield, Manchester are well worth a visit: Retail shop with cakes, chocolates and gifts, dining room where you can enjoy breakfast, lunch or afternoon tea (booking recommended). On the top floor is located our 'skills school' where we offer training in chocolate and sugar work. For a prospectus ring 0161 767 7766 or visit www.slattery.co.uk

Other very useful suppliers are:

Key Link
Chocolate ingredients, Packaging and Chocolate machinery.
www.keylink.org
Telephone 0114 245 5400

HB Ingredients
Chocolate and other ingredients
www.hbingredients.co.uk
Telephone 0844 324 4499

Home Chocolate Factory
Chocolate moulds, Chocolate ingredients
www.homechocolatefactory.com
Telephone 020 8450 1523

Meridian Speciality Packaging
Packaging and Boxes etc.
www.meridiansp.co.uk
Telephone 01684 578441

MSK Ingredients
Unusual and hard-to-find ingredients
www.msk-ingredients.com
Telephone 01246 412211

Party Plastics
Disposable plastic glasses
www.partyplastics.co.uk
Telephone 01753 664210

Cornish Cake Boards
Cake boards (bespoke sizes made to order), Cake decorations and sundries
www.cornishcakeboards.co.uk
Telephone 01872 572548

Knightsbridge PME
Cake decorations, tools and equipment
www.cakedecoration.co.uk
Telephone 020 3234 0049

Simply Ribbons
Ribbons of all types
www.simplyribbons.co.uk
Telephone 01691 780416

Chromos
Flexi curves, Artist brushes etc
www.chromosart.co.uk
Telephone 01227 638343

Nisbets
Knives, rolling pins etc
(next-day catering equipment)
www.nisbets.co.uk
Telephone 0845 140 5555

And of course, we sell many ingredients and tools:

197 Bury New Road
Whitefield
Manchester M45 6GE

www.slattery.co.uk
Telephone 0161 767 9303

Index

A

Alcohol
52 *Chocolate and Toffoc Soufflé*
70 *Drunken Chocolate Cake*

B

Bain-Marie
151 bain-marie

Base Cakes
156 base cakes

Basic Techniques
148 basic techniques

Biscuits
40 *Strawberry Shortbread Hearts*

Bread
50 *Chocolate and Pear, Bread and Butter Pudding*

Brownies
84 *Chocolate Pecan Brownies*

C

Cakes
164 cake, dowelling
162 cake, covering
160 cake, layering
163 cake, levelling
12 *Cake Pops*
76 *Chocolate and Coffee Cake*
80 *Chocolate Cupcakes*
84 *Chocolate Pecan Brownies*
70 *Drunken Chocolate Cake*

Centrepiece Cakes
88 *Agni Celebration Cake*
92 *Andora Celebration Cake*
96 *Bubble Celebration Cake*
134 *Darcy Celebration Cake*
101 *Fiona Celebration Cake*
104 *Georgia Celebration Cake*
108 *Julie Celebration Cake*
112 *Lola Celebration Cake*
116 *Olivia Celebration Cake*
141 *Shardé Celebration Cake*
120 *Suzie Celebration Cake*
126 *Tiffany Celebration Cake*
130 *Zandra Celebration Cake*

Cheesecake
58 *Double Chocolate Baked Cheesecake*

Chocolate
159 chocolate fudge filling
06 chocolate, history of
151 chocolate, melting
154 chocolate, moulds
158 chocolate paste
152 chocolate, pre-crystallising
159 chocolate, sauce
153 chocolate, testing
151 chocolate, tempering
08 chocolate, types
150 chocolate, working with

Cocoa Butter
151 cocoa butter

Cocoa Powder
32 *Chocolate Pecan Pie*
76 *Chocolate and Coffee Cake*
80 *Chocolate Cupcakes*
84 *Chocolate Pecan Brownies*
70 *Drunken Chocolate Cake*

Coffee
76 *Chocolate and Coffee Cake*

Confectionary
20 *Chocolate Baubles*
26 *White Chocolate Fudge*

Cranberry
24 *PCP (Pine Nut, Cranberry and Praline)*

D

Dark Chocolate
20 *Chocolate Baubles*
50 *Chocolate and Pear, Bread and Butter Pudding*
44 *Chocolate and Raspberry Cardinal*
52 *Chocolate and Toffoc Soufflé*
28 *Fruit and Nut Tiffin*
64 *Chocolate and Kumquat Semi Freddo*
80 *Chocolate Cupcakes*
54 *Chocolate Nemesis*
84 *Chocolate Pecan Brownies*
58 *Double Chocolate Baked Cheesecake*
70 *Drunken Chocolate Cake*
108 *Julie Celebration Cake*
40 *Strawberry Shortbread Hearts*

E

Equipment
146 equipment

F

Fudge
159 chocolate fudge filling
26 *White Chocolate Fudge*

Fruit
64 *Chocolate and Kumquat Semi Freddo*
44 *Chocolate and Raspberry Cardinal*
28 *Fruit and Nut Tiffin*

24 PCP (Pine Nut, Cranberry and Praline)
40 Strawberry Shortbread Hearts

G

Ganache
158 ganache for pouring or filling

K

Kumquat
64 Chocolate and Kumquat Semi Freddo

L

Lollipops
12 Cake Pops

M

Marzipan
162 marzipan, covering with

Microwave Oven
151 microwave oven

Milk Chocolate
20 Chocolate Baubles
96 Bubble Celebration Cake
12 Cake Pops
80 Chocolate Cupcakes
104 Georgia Celebration Cake
16 Manchester Tart Chocolates
34 Manchester Tart with a Chocolate Twist
141 Shardé Celebration Cake
40 Strawberry Shortbread Hearts
116 Olivia Celebration Cake
24 PCP (Pine Nut, Cranberry and Praline)
130 Zandra Celebration Cake

N

Nut
32 Chocolate Pecan Pie
28 Fruit and Nut Tiffin
24 PCP (Pine Nut, Cranberry and Praline)

P

Pear
50 Chocolate and Pear, Bread and Butter Pudding

Pecan
84 Chocolate Pecan Brownies
32 Chocolate Pecan Pie

Pie
32 Chocolate Pecan Pie

Pine nuts
24 PCP (Pine Nut, Cranberry and Praline)

Praline
24 PCP (Pine Nut, Cranberry and Praline)

Pudding
50 Chocolate and Pear, Bread and Butter Pudding
54 Chocolate Nemesis
60 Spiced Chocolate Pudding

R

Raspberry
44 Chocolate and Raspberry Cardinal

S

Shortbread
40 Strawberry Shortbread Hearts

Soufflé
52 Chocolate and Toffoc Soufflé

T

Tarts
44 Chocolate and Raspberry Cardinal
36 Chocolate Tarts
16 Manchester Tart Chocolates
34 Manchester Tart with a Chocolate Twist

Templates
168 Templates

Textures
165 Textures and curls

Torte
72 Chocolate Torte

W

White Chocolate
88 Agni Celebration Cake
92 Andora Celebration Cake
20 Chocolate Baubles
12 Cake Pops
134 Darcy Celebration Cake
58 Double Chocolate Baked Cheesecake
101 Fiona Celebration Cake
112 Lola Celebration Cake
116 Olivia Celebration Cake
120 Suzie Celebration Cake
126 Tiffany Celebration Cake
26 White Chocolate Fudge

Other titles available...

Whether it's a compilation of the very best chef talent or a dedicated cookbook of a chef's favourite recipes, discover our highly acclaimed cookbooks featuring some of the world's top chefs.

85 Inspirational Chefs £40.00

Relais & Châteaux chefs in North America, Mexico and The Carribbean reveal the recipes to their most desirable of dishes.

Chefs at Home £20.00

A compilation of the most-loved dishes chefs like to cook at home, using their favourite ingredients for quick bite and family recipes.

A World of Chocolate £25.00

A selection of recipes from chocolatiers and pâtissiers around the globe to celebrate the world's favourite ingredient.

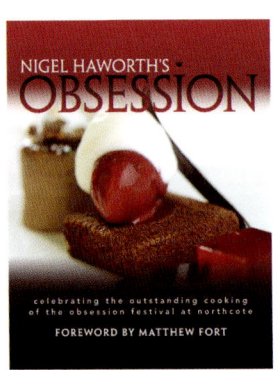

Nigel Haworth's Obsession £35.00

Michelin-starred Lancashire chef Nigel Haworth celebrates over 11 years of his Obsession festival with this compilation cookbook.

A Taste of Summer £25.00

Enjoy the taste of Summer with Brian Turner – including a range of dishes perfect for barbecues, desserts and even the odd rain shower!

Mark Jordan's Ocean Voyage £30.00

Michelin-starred Jersey based chef Mark Jordan shares his most mouthwatering recipes, as served in the Atlantic Hotel's Ocean Restaurant.

(Prices do not include postage and packaging)

For more information and to view other books in our collection visit...

www.chefmagazine.co.uk